Lieutenant Harry Loft

of Louth
and the 64th Regiment of Foot
(Second Staffordshire)

Martin Loft

Acknowledgements

I am grateful for the assistance I have received from the following:
The staff of the Regimental Museum of the Staffordshire Regiment, in helping with the background information about the 64th Regiment and in providing illustrations.
The Louth Antiquarians, Naturalists and Literary Society, especially their President, David Robinson OBE. for illustrations.
David Cuppleditch for permission to reproduce his painting of the Louth Mail Coach.
Diana Keene and my brother John Loft for illustrations and information about Ireland.
The staff of the Totley branch of Sheffield Library Service for their help in tracing books.

Especial thanks to my wife for looking after me in the 21st century while I have been living in the 19th.

The 64th Regiment of Foot (Second Staffordshire) amalgamated with the 98th Regiment of Foot and became the Prince of Wales's North Staffordshire Regiment on 1st July 1881

CHURNET VALLEY BOOKS
1 King Street, Leek, Staffordshire. ST13 5NW 01538 399033
thebookshopleek.co.uk

ISBN 1 897949 90 1

Printed and bound by Bath Press

CONTENTS

Old Louth c 1820

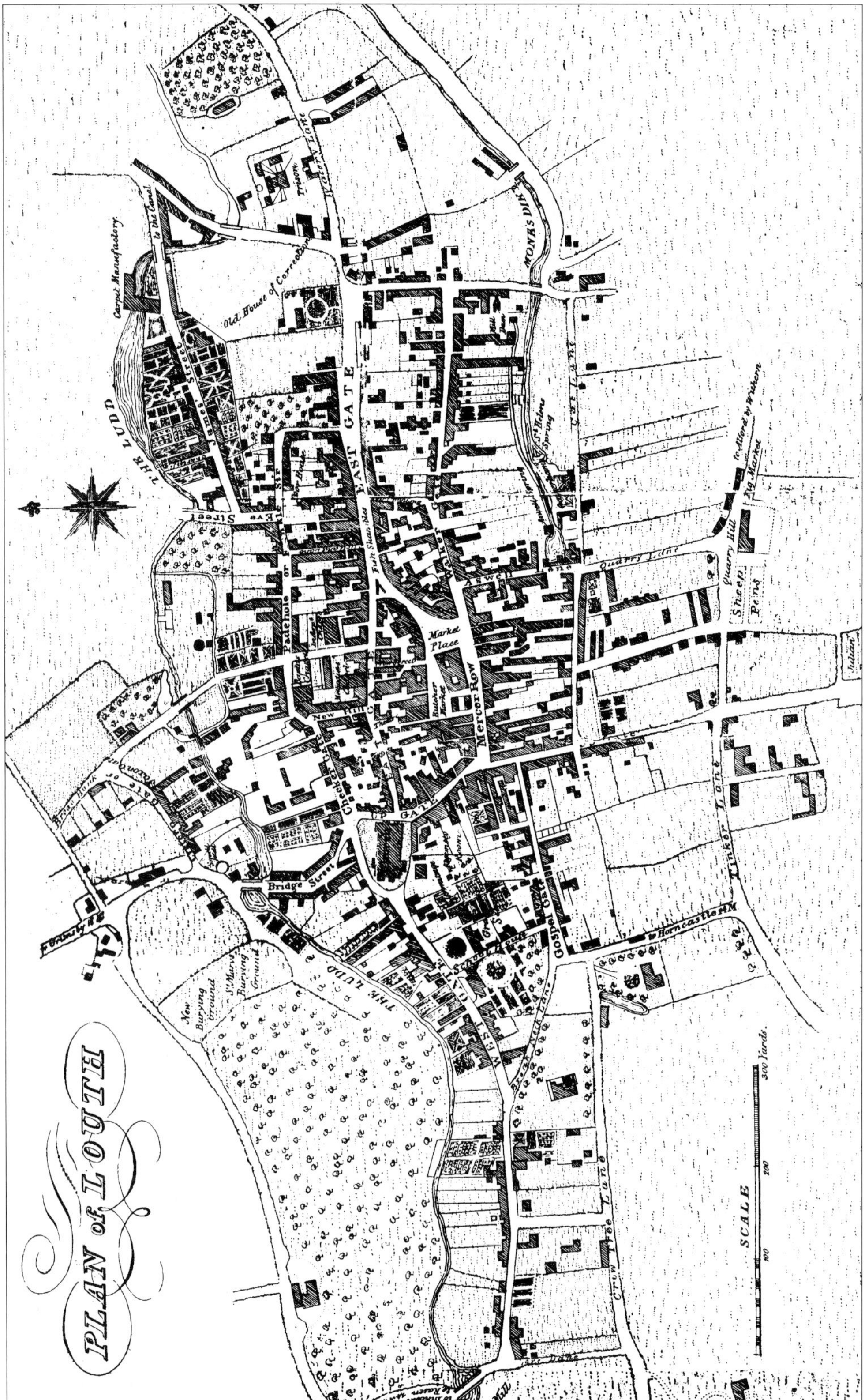

Map of Louth c. 1830

CHAPTER 1

HARRY'S HERITAGE

John Henry Capel Loft, 'Harry' to his friends, is the subject of our story. His grandfather, John Henry Loft, was from a farming family in the Marsh area of Lincolnshire but most unexpectedly joined the army and had a meteoric rise through the ranks of the Army, chiefly through his success in recruiting several thousand men for the war against France from his headquarters in Louth. In five years he was a Lieutenant Colonel, and eventually a Lieutenant General. He was much involved in the murky political scene in Grimsby, of which borough he was the Member of Parliament from 1808 until 1812, and he was a notable local antiquary.

A miniature of John Henry Loft, senior, in the uniform of a Lieutenant General in 1815.

A miniature of John Henry Loft, junior, as a Cornet in the I5th Hussars in 1815

Thomas Capel Loft was born in 1805, the General's fifth son by his wife Elizabeth. He was Harry's father. By 1825, his father, the General, was in 'financial' difficulties, but he still retained enough influence to obtain a commission for his "warm-hearted but impulsive" son. Thomas served with the 92nd Gordon Highlanders in Jamaica at a time when there was an almost complete collapse of regimental morale, largely due to yellow fever, known as "Yellow Jack". Thomas caught the disease, or as he put it in a letter to his mother *"I have been visited by Jacky"*, but he was one of the fortunate few to survive an attack. In 1827, he was still with the 92nd when they returned to their depot in Edinburgh Castle.

Thomas married Margaret Boswell (née Martin), a marriage that was both romantic but imprudent. Margaret's father, William Alexander Martin, was a

Grainthorpe Hall, the birthplace of John Henry Loft.

Harry's grandparents. John Henry Loft, "the old General", in his old age, and Elizabeth Loft. Elizabeth's portrait was painted after her death, from sketches.

Painted by Bennett Hubbard.

The Mansion in Westgate, Louth, where John Henry Loft lived while recruiting in the area during the Napoleonic War.

Edinburgh from the South. St. Cuthbert's Church, where Thomas and Margaret were married, to the left.

renowned writer of the day, the Writer to the Signet, and living in great style in the genteel surroundings of the New Town in Edinburgh. Margaret's mother died when Margaret was fifteen, leaving Margaret to assume some responsibility for her two brothers and one sister, with the help of many servants. Margaret had a distinguished career at Mr Scott's Academy for young ladies, winning many prizes for Writing, Arithmetic, English, French and Italian, and she was a prominent and popular member of Edinburgh society, with a very large circle of friends.

She was 17 when she met Thomas, but they had a guilty secret about the way in which they had become acquainted, for the truth was that they were never officially introduced. Thomas had apparently seen Margaret among the throng of young people in the Princes Street Gardens when the regimental band had been playing, and had been instantly attracted. He had contrived to make an opportunity to speak to her, and discovered that the attraction was mutual. They then started to meet regularly, giving the impression to Margaret's friends that Thomas was a friend of her family, and allowing her family to think that they had been introduced among the circle of her many acquaintances.

A view of the New Town in Edinburgh, where Margaret Loft was brought up, with Princes Street Gardens in the foreground, where she first met Thomas Loft.

Left: Alfred Wallis, the youngest son of John Henry and Elizabeth Loft. He was Harry's 'Uncle Fred'.

Right: John Henry Loft, junior, the eldest son of John Henry and Elizabeth Loft, and Harry's Uncle John.

It was all very innocent really, but nevertheless shocking in that genteel society. They would both have been mortified if the truth had become widely known. They met as often as Thomas's duty allowed, and frequently wrote to each other. In a short time they considered themselves to be informally engaged, though they realized that they would have to wait for years before they were married. When the 92nd was posted to Ireland they were both very despondent, but continued to write very affectionate letters and to exchange "likenesses" - silhouette portraits and also painted miniatures, which still survive.

Miniatures, painted in Edinburgh, of Thomas Loft and Margaret Martin, before they were married.

The first time Thomas went out shooting in Ireland, he discovered life there very different from that he had been familiar with in Lincolnshire, where he had been on equal and friendly terms with the farmers and their labourers. He wrote to Margaret:

*"I was walking with my gun and one of the Officers on Saturday last. I went into a field to some people cutting corn, and I asked them how much they had per day, and the answer was a shilling. And then they said if they had not had such a d*** bad king, they would not have such d*** bad laws. I said I would not listen to such Language and Treason. Then the firebrand again used such language, so I told him I considered it my duty to take him prisoner, having a double-barrelled gun in my hand. At which they said something in Irish which I could not understand, and after some black looks, and the other Officer coming up by this time, they changed the subject."*

The political situation in Ireland was volatile though there had been no widespread violence since the collapse of the United Irishmen's rising in 1798. Nevertheless there was considerable unrest, which found its expression in the gathering of nationalists in various societies under the general name of "Whiteboys". Thomas wrote:

"Last week about 30,000 of these reckless and foolish people, headed by a Mr. Lawless, sent to say that they would force their way into a town a few miles from here. In consequence of which some Horse and Foot were sent for and they prepared for action. The 30,000 thought it would be better to get away the best way they could and only one man of their party was killed. We have not yet heard what further took place. They usually only appear in large bodies where there are no troops. They have officers to command them, the same as we have - Majors, Captains and Subalterns, both infantry and cavalry. They do not like the Tartan, and whenever they see it they take themselves off, for they know we should stand on little ceremony with them."

On 30th September 1828 Thomas received some startling news from Edinburgh. Margaret's father had died very suddenly, at the age of 48, of *"a paralytic affliction"*. Moreover the family had made the terrible discovery that he was bankrupt; there was not enough money to pay his creditors, and Margaret, her sister Christina, and her brothers Peter and William, were literally penniless. An aunt in Edinburgh took them in temporarily but their future was very bleak!

Thomas felt more despondent and helpless than ever, but after a few months of negotiations he came back to Edinburgh, and married Margaret at St. Cuthbert's Church, Newington, on 23rd February 1829. Officers usually did not marry until they had reached the rank of Captain, in command of a Company. Thomas was still only an Ensign, with no income beyond his pay, and Margaret had no income at all. Margaret's friends thought it was a highly romantic and most gentlemanly act on Thomas's part, proving *"that his attachment was entirely disinterested"*. It seems possible that the marriage was something of a relief to Margaret's relations, who were unable or unwilling to take responsibility for the orphaned young people.

After the wedding Thomas and Margaret, and her sister Christina, joined the Regiment in Ireland and were blissfully happy, sometimes in barracks and sometimes out in the country on detachment, which was the normal method of placement for the Army, keeping as wide an area as possible under control. Margaret kept very careful accounts to make sure that their very small income went as far as possible.

On 13th January 1830 their happiness increased when their first child, Harry, was born at Carlow, where the regiment was stationed. At his baptism on 21st March 1830, by the Rector of Carlow, he was given the names John Henry after his grandfather, the old General, and Capel after his father. His godparents were Captain George Thorold, Thomas's Company Commander, John Vigors, a fellow-officer, and Mrs Carey, John Vigor's sister. Strangely both Thomas Loft and George Thorold came from old Lincolnshire families in a regiment that was almost entirely Scottish.

Thomas and Margaret's happiness was short lived. Six months later Thomas was taken ill. In spite of the attention of Dr. Anderson, the regimental surgeon, his condition did not improve and it was thought that the disease had *'settled on his lungs'*. In the face of some opposition, and in spite of the considerable expense involved, Thomas determined to go on sick leave to his family home at Healing in Lincolnshire, where he was convinced he had the best chance of making a complete recovery.

Just before they left, Thomas and Margaret picked a bunch of wild flowers, which Margaret pressed, and kept among her treasures for the rest of her life. They still survive although now only a few dusty stems in an envelope on which Margaret wrote *"Gathered with my beloved husband at Nenagh in August 1830"*.

They made the long journey by packet boat and stagecoach to Healing, where Thomas's mother, Elizabeth Loft, was living with her relations. It was the first time that Margaret had met any of Thomas's family, but they made her warmly welcome, once they saw how devoted she was to their *"dear Tom"*. She found herself living among people she did not know, living in a way that was completely strange to her, in an unfamiliar country. Until this point in her life she had only known either a very comfortable existence in a large thriving city, surrounded by her family and lifelong friends, or the close-knit community of the Regiment, with a very orderly pattern of life, in which she had found much support and affection.

Healing itself was a small village with about 100 inhabitants, rather off the beaten track, without a shop or an inn. The nearest town was Grimsby, which was not much more than a large village at the time. The nearest large town with communications to the rest of the country was Hull on the other side of the Humber. The Lofts occupied two houses, one managed by Elizabeth Loft and the other by her sister Lucy Farr, where they lived a rather chaotic life, with continual bickering among Thomas's brothers, who were much more concerned with leading a sporting life than with earning a living. It was not unusual for eight members of the two households to ride out of the stables to a meet of the Brocklesby Hunt.

Old Louth, c1845

For a short time Thomas seemed to have rallied a little and managed to join in the family activities but his constitution had been weakened by the yellow fever, and he died at Healing on 7th April 1831, aged 25. Margaret, still only 21 years old, was six months pregnant, and gave birth to their second son, James Edmund Wallis Loft, on 28th July in the same year. A slight consolation in her grief was the fact that shortly before his death Thomas was promoted to Lieutenant. She would therefore receive a slightly larger pension, of £62 a year.

Margaret's immediate problem was to find somewhere to live on her small pension. Healing was too crowded and could not provide the atmosphere and facilities which Margaret thought necessary for bringing up her children. Her own relations in Scotland offered no encouragement for her to return to her native country, which had been Margaret's first natural inclination.

Happily some old family friends of the Lofts came to her help. The Revd. Edmund Smyth found her a suitable partly furnished cottage at an annual rent of £10 in the village of South Elkington, just outside Louth, where his brother, the Revd. William Smyth, was the Rector. The Revd William lived in the Hall, and was the owner of most of the land in the parish. Edmund was the Vicar of North Elkington but lived in the Rectory at South Elkington. Elkington was a small village but it was only about 2 miles from Louth, and could provide the facilities that Margaret was looking for as well as a wider range of acquaintances than could be found at Healing. Edmund Smyth's wife was about Margaret's age and they soon became very good friends. Moreover the Smyths invited Margaret to stay with them as their guest for a few weeks while she was getting her affairs sorted out. So it was in Elkington that her new baby was christened James Edmund Wallis Loft; James Wallis after his uncle and godfather, and Edmund after Edmund Smyth. On 24th October 1831 she moved into her new home with her two small sons.

Louth Parish Church from Westgate - little changed since Harry knew it.

CHAPTER 2

HARRY'S CHILDHOOD

With the help of her new kind friends, and with her own indomitable courage, Margaret set about the task of bringing up her two sons. The cottage contained a sitting room, two bedrooms, a kitchen and a dairy. The only furniture was two bedsteads, 6 chairs and two tables. Margaret managed gradually to acquire what else she needed. Some cases of her possessions from Edinburgh eventually arrived at the Riverhead in Louth, almost intact, having travelled by sea to Hull, and then in a sloop across the Humber and up the Louth Navigation canal at a total cost of £1.10.10.

Keddington Lock, Louth Canal, c. 1850. *Courtesy of Louth Navigation Trust.*

The family settled down to a quiet life with no great upheavals. The boys both suffered from the usual childish illnesses, but on the whole they were healthy, though James, usually known as Jamie or Jem, was always the more robust and sturdy. Most years they were invited to join the Smyths for a holiday at Mablethorpe, and they sometimes stayed with relations at Hull and with friends at Binbrook or Grainthorpe, but it was the visits to Healing that really mattered to the boys.

During this time Margaret's elder brother, Peter Martin, had been a young officer with the army of the East India Company. She had corresponded with him but because of the time it took for the mail to go to India, neither of them was ever up to date with each other's news. In April 1832 Margaret received yet another shock. She received a letter from an aunt:

"We have received most distressing accounts from India. You have been

supported through many severe trials and I trust fortitude will be granted to you at this time, to bear with meekness and patience the will of God. We have heard from a friend that your dear brother Peter is no more. He had been in bad health for some time, and was sent to the mountains for recovery. He got quite well but on return to Quarters he incautiously exposed himself to the sun and caught a fever which carried him off, last October."

Peter was just 22 years old, and had been in India for three years, having left Edinburgh when his father was apparently prosperous and in good health.

So in six years Margaret had lost her parents, her husband and her brother. Meanwhile her younger brother, William Martin, had gone to Tobago where at the age of sixteen he had been given the post of Overseer on a sugar plantation, still worked by slave labour.

Sometimes the news from Scotland was much more welcome. In 1835 both Margaret and Christina received a legacy from a Miss Campbell of Ayr, who had employed Christina as a companion. This allowed Christina to travel to Margaret at Elkington, where there was a rapturous reunion for the two sisters who had not met since their departure from Ireland. She stayed with her sister over Christmas when they spent a wonderful few days at Healing.

Margaret wrote to her brother William. *"We were a very large party, 12 or 13 sitting down to dinner every day. There were six of my brothers-in-law, who are all musical, so what with singing, playing the Piano, Flute, Violin and Bugle, with Quadrilles and Waltzing, and a Round game every evening, we passed the time very pleasantly. They all have such good spirits, and are so merry and happy among themselves. There is a very great likeness throughout the Family, indeed you may easily tell a Loft among a dozen young men, as they all have something special about them, which I cannot describe. You may laugh at me but this is what everybody says. Christina carried on a violent flirtation with Henry, the fifth son. Harry gets every day more and more like the Family."* Christina remembered how *"the dear chaps sang Zuyder Zee and The Jolly Red Nose".*

At this time the Loft brothers ranged in age from John, aged thirty-eight, to Fred, aged nineteen. Sometimes the brothers came to stay at Elkington, usually for the shooting. In 1836 William Loft was brought there in an emergency because he had sustained concussion and severe bruising, following a fall from his horse in the Louth Steeplechase. Margaret commented *"It will not deter him from riding again as he is determined to show them what he can do some day soon."* There were some years and many falls to go before William's determination was vindicated.

A more frequent visitor was the youngest of the Loft brothers, Alfred Arthur, known as Uncle Fred to his nephews. In spite of being the youngest of the family he had inherited the Healing estate from his grandfather, on condition that he adopted the surname Wallis. This inevitably caused difficulties with the other brothers. Being the nearest to them in age he was Harry and Jem's favourite uncle, and took a close interest in all their affairs. From his correspondence it is evident that having been fond of Margaret as a sister-in-law since they first met, his attachment gradually grew into something more passionate.

At that time there could be no question of marriage between them, because it was still illegal to marry a deceased brother's widow. It is impossible to determine just what were Margaret's feelings towards Fred, since there are no letters from her to him, though a great many of his to Margaret have survived. He was six years younger than Margaret, which was no doubt the reason why some of his earliest letters are addressed to *"my dear old woman",* but gradually that was replaced by *"my dearest Margaret", "My dearest Kitten"*, and finally by *"My own Pet".* His attachment to her caused him to be very jealous of any attention paid to her by other men, particularly his own brothers, and it survived at least until his marriage in 1848.

At a slightly later date, another Louth couple found themselves in almost the same position but they pursued it further. Susanna Allison, the wife of William Allison, a solicitor and a prominent figure in the community, died in 1846 leaving William with seven children to care for. He was greatly helped following his loss by his sister-in-law, and in 1848 they wanted to be married. Since this was impossible in England they travelled to Prussia where they believed the law allowed such a marriage. Unfortunately they found this was not the case, and had to return to Louth, to their own great embarrassment, where they were met by the sympathy of their friends and by the amusement of some others. The Allison boys, particularly the eldest, Faulkner, became great friends of Harry and Jem Loft, though they always knew him as Faulk.

Margaret undertook the boys' education herself, with the help of Edmund Smyth. By the time Harry was six she reported to her brother:

"I give them a good long lesson every day. Harry is a quick sensible boy, so it is quite an amusement for him. He has been reading a book on astronomy, which pleases him very much. He knows the capitals of all the countries on the map, also the island of Tobago where Uncle Willy lives! He can do a long sum in Addition very well, and various other accomplishment too numerous to be related!

He was highly delighted in the winter, as Mr. Smyth has two large ponds and during the frost Mr. S. kindly gave him a pair of skates. To my great amazement there he was flying over the ice. I could hardly believe my eyes! Of course he had a good many tumbles at first, but he soon got over them, as he does not care about a bump or two. He is very active with very much his poor father's figure. He is now 4 feet 10 inches, and promises to be very tall. Jamie is very like our family, very healthy with such fine rosy cheeks, and such a laughing good-humoured countenance. He reads and spells little words very nicely, is very steady and sedate, but quick at his books."

It was at about this time that Jem had his first experience of cricket. In his old

Ice-skating, cricket and horseracing in the 1840s from the Illustrated London News.

age he often recounted the story. *"At the age of five I stood at the crease for the first time and faced Harry's bowling. The first ball was perilously close to my head, and the second one hit me on the nose, which bled profusely. Mr. Smyth came to my rescue and held me under the pump, and I was sent to bed."* Nevertheless Jem went on to be one of the most enthusiastic cricketers in a cricket-loving family.

The time came when Margaret realized that Harry was old enough to need more education than he could get at home. She explained the position in a letter to her brother William:

"Harry is now old enough to go to School which requires a residence in Louth to entitle the boys to go free of expense. Is it not a capital thing for me? They receive an excellent Classical education, and have the very best masters; the books are the only expense, and something on entrance. It will be a very great change for me, but the thought that it is for my dear boys' good will reconcile me to many deprivations which in a Town, with a very limited income, I must expect to have."

Margaret was correct in her estimate of the School's reputation, though the methods employed to achieve academic success were ruthless. Since 1814 the Headmaster had been the Reverend John Waite, a former pupil of the School, who had built up both the numbers and the standard of education, firmly based upon the classical tradition, to a remarkable degree. He was said to have *'cultivated irascibility with great care for many years. His temper was partly by nature, partly by principle, of a highly inflammatory kind'.* Sixty years later one of his former pupils admitted that the thought of *"Waite and that fiendish cane"* still haunted him.

One of Waite's pupils was Alfred Tennyson, whose memories of the School were so distasteful to him that he would never walk past it in his later life. His younger brothers had been fellow pupils of Harry Loft's uncles. Fortunately the Usher, the Reverend Thomas Aquila Dale, commonly known as 'Piggy' to his pupils, was of a gentler disposition than the Headmaster. One of his favourite threats was *"Boy, I will give you a sad rap",* but it was not very effective when he had to compete with Waite's thunderings from the other end of the School Room. Sometimes when their return to Louth after a holiday had been delayed by some mischance, Harry and his brother James were alarmed at what the Headmaster's reaction would be, but Margaret's epistolary skill usually averted any major catastrophe, as when she wrote to Mr. Waite: *"Mrs. Loft presents her kind regards to Mr. Waite, and as Mrs. Iles has been so good as to ask her boys to go to Binbrook this afternoon, after School, Mrs. Loft will feel exceedingly obliged if Mr. Waite will kindly allow them to do so. Mrs. Loft begs to return her most sincere thanks for Mr Waite's very great kindness and consideration to her Boys."* When faced with an approach of this kind, even Waite's heart must have melted.

The Reverend John Waite, Headmaster of Louth Grammar School when Harry and Jem were pupils.

In fact Harry started at the Grammar School just before the family left Elkington. Margaret wrote:

"As Elkington is only two and a half miles from Louth he walks backwards and forwards. He is a remarkably good boy. He gets up every morning at 7, sets off at 8 to be at School for 9. He has his dinner in Louth, and leaves School again at 5, so he has plenty of it. He does not dislike it at all, and is making good progress."

On 17th May 1837 Margaret and the boys moved to their new house in Lee Street in Louth. She wrote to William: *"I have found a house, which is a nice one though a little dark and cramped, after living in the country, and the rent is rather more than I ought to give. It has a nice piece of playground for the boys. I shall try it for a year, and if my expenses exceed my income I shall have to move to a smaller house, but the thought that it is for my boys' good will reconcile me to many deprivations, which in a Town with a very limited income I must expect to have."*

Margaret missed the company of Edmund and Ann Smyth, but very quickly became a close friend of Ann's sister, Susan Banks, the wife of Dr John Banks. When the doctor was out on his rounds Susan was very glad of Margaret's company at their house in Upgate, very close to Lee Street. The fact that John and Mary had two sons, Charlie and Henry, of similar ages to Harry and Jem, made the bond between them even closer. Even when the Doctor moved into a new and splendid house at Stewton,

Lee Street, Louth, where Margaret Loft lived when she and her sons first came to Louth, probably in one of the houses on the left.

on the outskirts of the town, Margaret walked over to see Susan several times a week.

They made a great many friends, chiefly among the professional families in the town, and some of the farming families in the neighbourhood, and entered into their social life and entertainments. As an attractive and well-educated young woman, Margaret was a welcome addition to society among such people, especially as she bore a name that had been well known in the district for many years. Moreover, she was often in demand as a chaperone for the daughters of her friends at concerts, dances and other amusements.

Harry was a hard-working scholar and became Head Boy. He was regarded as a good influence on his contemporaries. After he left Louth his friend Charley Banks wrote to him saying: *"I often think of how you used to help me with my verses, and how I looked up to you as the nimblest and strongest boy in the School".*

Lizzie Lundie, a cousin of Thomas Loft, wrote to Margaret from Hull saying: *"We often talk of your dear boys, and you must forgive me if I declare in favour of Harry. James is a dear little fellow and a nice pet, but there is something about Harry quite irresistible. Depend upon it; he will make wild work with many a poor girl's heart some day, for he has quite that kind of fascination. He is a great deal older than his years."*

Harry and his brother learned from their mother to value gentility above all other virtues. Margaret's most damning assessment of a man's character was to say, *"He is not a gentleman".* It was not merely a matter of breeding, nor was it solely to do with etiquette, for Harry sometimes described as *"a gentlemanly fellow"* a person who was *"rough"* in some aspects, but who showed courtesy and a proper consideration of others' feelings. On the other hand Margaret accepted that John Bell, a Militia officer in Louth, was a gentleman, while pouring scorn upon him for being known as Lieutenant instead of plain Mister, which would never have happened in the Gordon Highlanders

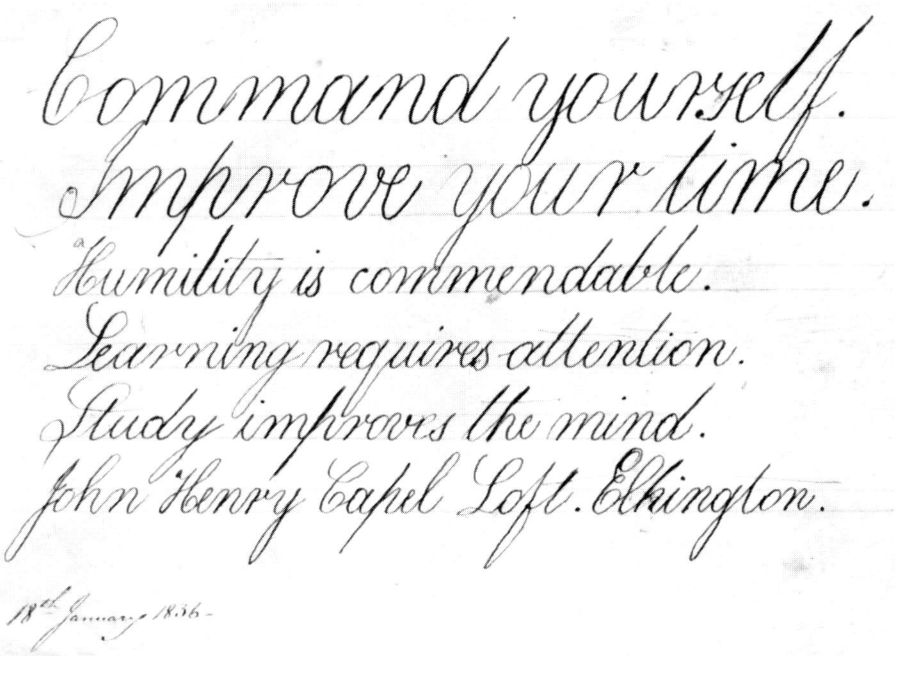

Copper plate writing by Harry Loft at the age of 6, as taught to him by his mother.

Harry and James enjoyed a wide range of activities with their friends in the town. They were enthusiastic cricketers, but apparently never played football. The boys' greatest delight was to stay at Healing with their grandmother, where their uncles encouraged them to take part in country sports, in a rough and ready way. There were horses to ride, rough shooting, coursing, wildfowling, swimming, skating, and fishing. Sometimes when they had a day's holiday from school they would leave home early in the morning, walk the 12 miles to Grainsby, where Uncle Fred kept his horses, for a day's sport, and then walk home at night. If they were lucky they might get a lift for part of the way on one of the coaches, from a friendly driver. Their uncle William Loft's determination paid off when he won the Grand National on his horse Cure-all in 1845, and the boys often organized steeplechases in the fields round Louth, in which the competitors entered under the name of a horse. Harry was always Cure-all.

William Loft on Cure-all, the winner of the 1845 Grand National, painted by Bennett Hubbard.

A self-portrait of Bennett Hubbard, the Louth artist who painted the portraits of John Henry and Elizabeth Loft, and the painting of William Loft on Cure-all.

Interior of Louth Parish Church today. In Margaret Loft's time there were 'free' benches in the centre and 'private' box pews each side.

On Sundays, Margaret and the boys went to the Parish Church of St. James, which was flourishing under the direction of the Reverend E. R. Mantell. They usually went twice, for Matins and Evensong. About once a month Margaret *'stayed the Sacrament'* as she called her attendance at Holy Communion. At first they sat in the free benches in the middle of the Church, but in 1845 they acquired a pew of their own, much to Margaret's gratification.

When Harry was twelve Margaret began to think about his future, and consulted anyone who might be able to help. Captain John Davern, an old friend from the 92nd Regiment and a veteran of Waterloo, wrote to her from Chelsea College:

"You ask my advice as to your making application to Lord Hill in behalf of your son. I have no hesitation in recommending your so doing, but you must be aware that he has no other situation to give but that of the Army. Your Memorial should be as strong as possible, stating all particulars, backed if possible by a Conservative Member of Parliament or a General Officer. Send it to The Rt. Honourable Lord Hill, under cover to Lord Fitzroy Somerset, with a note requesting he will be so kind as to lay it before the General Commanding in Chief for his consideration. Your claim is a just one, and you are nothing worse should you be unsuccessful. I don't see any occasion to mention that your boys are educated at a free school, but you must act as you think proper.

Colonel MacDonald is at Barbados, but he would no doubt vouch for the correctness of your Statement. Winchester and Mrs. W. were here about a month ago on their return from the West Indies, and are gone to Scotland, where he will be at Fort George, commanding the Depot. I am sure he would give you any assistance in his power. You should leave nothing untried, and make use of all the interest and support you can. The young man would not be gazetted under 16 years, but you will be fortunate to get his name on the list, as the applications at present are numerous. I must tell you that Lord Fitzroy Somerset is a very considerate and good man."

Lord Hill had been one of the Duke of Wellington's Generals in the Peninsula, and was known to his troops as Daddy Hill, because of his concern for their welfare. Lord Fitzroy Somerset had been an aide to the Duke at Waterloo and lost his right arm in the battle. Later, as Lord Raglan, he was the commander of the British forces in the Crimean War.

Colonel John MacDonald had seen a lot of action in the Peninsular War, commanding a Portuguese regiment, as well as taking part in the disastrous attack on Buenos Ayres. In 1828 he had taken command of the 92nd. Major Winchester had joined the 92nd in 1805, and had fought with the Regiment in the Peninsular, as well as at Quatre Bras and Waterloo, where he had been severely wounded. He had been Acting Lieutenant Colonel when the Regiment returned from Jamaica, and most of the officers had hoped that his appointment would be made permanent, and so were disappointed when Col. MacDonald got the position. Mrs Winchester had been very kind to Margaret during her time in Ireland.

Antigua. Both the 64th and the 38th (Staffordshire regiments) spent a lot of the late 18th and early 19th centuries in the West Indies, as Britain, France and Spain sought to cut up the spoils. (see Ch 1)

Margaret followed Captain Davern's advice and left nothing untried. She wrote to everybody she could think of who might be of some assistance. Each letter was drafted in rough, sometimes three times, before being written in her finest copperplate, and in the most correct language. Colonel MacDonald, Lieutenant-Colonel Winchester, Major Thorold, and Captain Sutherland were all approached, but she put most hope in enlisting the support of General Sir John MacDonald, the Adjutant General, whose niece had been one of Margaret's friends in Edinburgh. The formal application was sent to Lord Fitzroy Somerset on 27th May, and on 13th June a reply came to say that Lord Hill had put Harry's name on his list for a commission, without purchase, after he had attained the prescribed age.

Margaret was delighted by the news. Her brother, William Martin, now the Manager of the sugar plantation in Tobago, had been a generous uncle to Harry, and Margaret at once wrote to him:

"Although not exactly what I should have preferred for my Boy, as there are so many temptations in a soldier's life and they are exposed to many vicissitudes, it will be a provision and a gentlemanly one too. When the time comes, perhaps, if Lord George Murray, my Countryman, should succeed the Duke of Wellington, as I am told is possible, I shall have interest sufficient to get Harry appointed to the 92nd which from being his poor Father's Regiment and having both his godfather's Captains in it, of course I should very much prefer."

Although it would be about four years before Harry would actually receive his commission, Margaret wanted to ensure that he was prepared as well as possible for his Army career, so another series of letters was sent, about the best way of ensuring this. *"I should very much like him to learn the Modern languages, Military Drawing, etc. which I fancy would be of more especial service than devoting all his time to Latin and Greek. I am glad to say that he is making considerable progress in both of these. I met the Headmaster, the Revd. Mr Waite the other day, who gave me a most favourable account of both my Boys, and said they were as good as, if not better than, any in the School."*

She thought that the new Royal Military College at Sandhurst might be possible, although most of her correspondents assured her that boys learned just as much at any good school and made just as good officers. However she did write to Sir John Saville, the Commandant of the College, for details, including the possibility of reduced fees for a person in Harry's position. His reply was not very encouraging, and when she discovered that it would cost at least £100 a year, she abandoned the idea. However she did write annually to the War Office, to make sure that they had not forgotten Harry.

Meanwhile life in Louth continued in its usual way, with Margaret and the boys increasing the circle of their friends each year, and making their accustomed round of visits. In the winter of 1840 the boys visited their uncle and aunt, James and Mary Loft, in Hull, where their cousins, the Lundie family, also lived.

Robert Lundie was Governor of the prison at Hull. His wife, Mary, reported to Margaret, *"I never saw boys enjoy themselves as much as your two do with us at present."* Lizzie Lundie wrote to Margaret about the visit:

"We had great excitement and alarm when your boys were with us the other day. As you may know, in the case of a debtor escaping from the prison the Governor becomes responsible for all his debts. So you may imagine the consternation there was during this time when one such prisoner escaped, as the sum involved was a very large one. The prison staff started an intensive search of the district, which at first was unproductive. However one of the turnkeys went to the inn where the London mail coach was on the point of leaving. He looked inside the coach, spotted the escaping prisoner, dressed in female clothing, and apprehended him. Their triumphant return to the prison was the signal for great rejoicing by all of us."

The Christmas of 1845 was the last that Margaret and her sons would enjoy together for some years. They celebrated New Year at Healing with a series of parties. The New Year's Eve Quadrille party at Mr John Bell's house was attended by over 50 people, including ten Lofts, and lasted until 5 am. There was *"an exceedingly pleasant evening of music and dancing at the Iles's house"*, and similar parties at the Masons's house and at Healing House itself, all finishing in the small hours of the morning. On 2nd January Margaret watched with pride as Harry and Jem set off on two of their uncle's horses for a meet of the Brocklesby Hunt, at which Jem rode so well that he was commended by the Huntsman.

The visit ended in anticlimax, as they returned to Louth by carrier's cart on a bitterly cold day:

"We stopped at 1 pm for refreshments at the inn at Grainsby, and resumed our miserably slow journey, which was only enlivened by meeting many of our friends returning from the Wednesday market at Louth. At the top of the Grimsby Road hill the horse was stumbling badly from the frost and snow, so the carrier had to lead it down the hill, which caused me intense consternation. After a tedious journey of over six hours the cart deposited us at the bottom of Lee Street, very thankful to be safely home."

On 20th April 1846 Harry received a letter from the Adjutant General announcing that The Duke of Wellington, now Commander-in-Chief for life, had granted him a commission, without purchase. It was in the 64th Regiment of Foot, the North Staffordshire Regiment, which he was to join in Ireland on 31st May. This was cause for great rejoicing, and congratulations poured in from all Margaret's correspondents, though many of them recognised that she would feel sad at the approaching separation. Harry's godfather, Major George Thorold of the 92nd,

A Meet of the Southwold Hunt at Elkington Hall, the home of the Smythe family, who were good friends of Margaret Loft.

A painting, by David Cuppleditch, of the Mail Coach leaving Louth for London. Harry agreed with a coachman who said that a drive on the top of a coach would do much more good than a great many doctors - but not on a day like this.

wrote to express his pleasure at the news, to give good advice to his godson, and to say *"I cannot offer him a better wish than that he may follow the example of his father, for whom I had a very great regard, and as he was in my Company all the time we were together in the Regiment I knew him better than anyone."*

There was also cause for concern because the cost of uniform and equipment was considerable, even though Margaret obtained quotations from various London firms before placing any orders. Most of the firms approached could offer a full uniform for about £50, though this did not include ordinary wearing apparel or linen, or such things as a portable iron bedstead, chair, chest, wash-stand, etc. costing about the same. Each firm sought custom by offering very competitive prices, and also by giving references from their satisfied clients, in one case the Adjutant of the 64th, and in another Mr. William Loft of Trusthorpe, a distant relation of Thomas Loft. Captain John Davern, who had been helpful in advising Margaret how to apply for a commission, now gave advice on what was absolutely essential, and what could be bought later.

Margaret and Harry went to London where eventually Margaret drove a hard bargain with Thomas Shotter of Jermyn Street to supply all Harry's uniform, and other clothes, including a black Dress Coat and a Shooting Coat with trousers and waistcoats to match. Harry remembered the journey well. They travelled from Peterborough to London by train in a 2nd class coach, but between Peterborough and Louth they went by coach, since the railway had not reached Louth. Harry wrote about the journey home a year later.

"What a beautiful morning it was. The old coachman said that a drive on the top of a coach on a day like that would do people much more good than a great many doctors, and I agreed with him. I was tired enough of the railway."

The Louth firm of Campbell, Bowmar and Ranshaw received the

A train from the 1840s - actually carrying Queen Victoria here.

Louth Station, opened in 1849. Margaret Loft travelled from Louth to New Holland in the Directors' train, the day before the official opening of the line.

order for much of Harry's linen. A rather unexpected account was with George Warner, a licensed Hawker from Horncastle, who supplied vests and 'pantelooms'.

There were all sorts of other items to be acquired. It was necessary to have visiting cards, correctly engraved, and an appropriate card case, a writing case fully supplied with stationery, a dressing case, and books. On this last subject Harry asked for advice from the Adjutant of the 64th, as he had some books that he thought might be adequate, which his uncle James, a half-pay Lieutenant in the Fusiliers, had given him. The Adjutant replied: *"The books you mention appear to be of such very old date that they will be of no use whatever. You must therefore provide yourself with ones of more recent publication. I also beg to inform you that under the existing stringent regulations, no Shell Jacket of any description is permitted to be worn in the 64th Regiment. Officers are therefore obliged to appear at their Mess in full Dress Coatee."* So that was one item less to be bought, and £3 saved.

However friends and relations were very generous. As soon as he heard the news William Martin, whom Harry had never yet met, sent £100 from Tobago, and Harry's uncle, James Wallis Loft, remembering his own days as an impecunious Ensign in the 7th Fusiliers, promised him £20, on condition that he did not spend any of it until he had spent at least one night in barracks. He also sent a lot of advice to Margaret, suggesting that it might be advantageous for Harry to leave the Grammar School and have special instruction in subjects like mathematics and history, which would be of advantage to him in his new profession. He added:

"No doubt you will be as proud of Harry as my poor mother was when John

came home for the first time in full uniform. Old Mrs. Walesby said, 'Look at her; she brounges about as proud as a peacock, and says to all the mothers she meets, Look at mine! Have you got such a one?" I am afraid Harry has none of the advantages that John had, but he's a fine fellow, none the less".

Harry's godfather, Major Thorold, sent some money, as did his aunt, Miss Thorold, who lived in Louth. Another uncle, Fred, already mentioned, made a substantial contribution. Other friends also helped, so eventually Harry was very well equipped.

At this time, aged just 16, he was a little under six feet tall, rather slender, weighing about 11 stone, with the curly auburn hair which appeared in both his father's and his mother's families. He had visited Edinburgh and London but his knowledge of the world was largely limited to his experience of a market town and the surrounding villages, in a district which was rather cut off from the general life of the nation. His education at the Grammar School had been a strictly classical one, much more restricted than that of his Scottish mother, who had learned French and Italian and had received prizes for mathematics. It seems from a reference in one of Harry's letters that he may have attended Campbell's Military Academy in Edinburgh, but it can only have been for a short time. In any case, his boyhood had now finished.

The old Louth Grammar School in School House Lane, as it was when Harry and Jem were pupils.

CHAPTER THREE

HARRY'S COMMISSION

The unit in which Harry had been commissioned, the 64th Regiment of Foot, had returned to England from Nova Scotia in 1845. It then travelled from Southampton to Wedon in Northamptonshire by train, covering 154 miles in just a few hours, which must have seemed miraculous to most of the men. Until this time the army considered ten miles a day to be a reasonable speed for infantry in full marching order. They now moved to Ireland and had to get accustomed to marching everywhere once again. The Regimental Headquarters were set up in barracks in Kilkenny, though as was the usual custom for regiments in Ireland, various companies were spread across the district on detachment so that they could deal with any disturbance that might arise.

Harry's life in Ireland with the 64th, either in barracks or on detachment, was very similar to that of his father, Thomas Loft, with the 92nd Highlanders, 20 years previously. The granting of the vote to some Catholics in 1832 (Peel's Catholic Emancipation Act) had made some improvement to the political situation, but the failure of the potato harvest in 1845 had caused the greatest difference, since it made strictly political considerations irrelevant. Any unrest was now due to the local economic situation, and took the form of food riots, or protests at the policy of the landowners - who were attempting to force the peasant population to leave their land and become paid labourers - rather than full-scale rebellion.

Moreover the 64th, since their return to England, had been equipped with percussion rifles, an improvement on the flintlock muskets used by the 92nd in 1830. This fact must have made the possibility of any serious armed rising less likely. It is notable that whereas his father said that he and his fellow-officers were always armed when out of barracks, Harry seemed to be able to walk unarmed and on his own, wherever he liked.

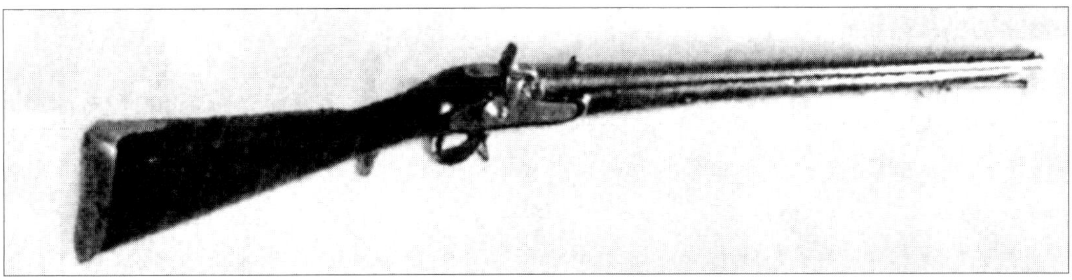

An 1842 pattern British percussion rifle *Courtesy of Dave Cooper*

In his letters Harry seems to have written as much about the weather, and his happy memories of former years, as he did about his military activities. It may be that, as he knew his mother had experienced regimental life at first hand, she would not need to be told about the normal routine in the army.

In May 1846 Margaret and Harry left Louth for Ireland. It would be another two years before the railway reached Louth, so they caught the tide-coach to Grimsby, so called because it was timed to reach Grimsby at high tide, rather than running to a timetable. They took the steam packet to Hull, from where they went by train to Liverpool on the recently opened railway. They then crossed to Ireland, going first to Carlow, Harry's birthplace, where they stayed for a few days with Harry's godmother, Mrs. Carey and her husband, who had been friends of Margaret in her days with the 92nd Regiment. It must have been very strange, and sad, for Margaret, as she found herself once again in the surroundings where she had spent those few happy months with her husband, Thomas, before his health broke down. Then Harry went to Kilkenny, where he reported to the barracks as a very junior Ensign. In the first of his many letters as an officer to his mother, he described joining his Regiment:

1st July 1846

"I did not arrive at Kilkenny until seven o'clock. I left my boxes at the Victoria Hotel and went up to the Barracks, where I asked for the Adjutant's Quarters. The Adjutant was at Mess, so I went back to the Hotel till 8.30 pm, when I went back to the Barracks. But they were still in the Mess drinking their wine. I was walking about when the Mess waiter came running up and asked if my name was Loft, and told me that Mr. Carter, the Adjutant, would see me at the Mess. He came out and shook hands with me, and asked me to go into the Mess, where he introduced me to the other officers. I sat down and had a glass of wine with them, and then Mr. C. took me to the Colonel, who had been away for a week and had only that minute returned. He is a very nice person, and is much liked. He asked me if I had come straight from England, and a few other things, and then spoke to Mr. C. about the Regiment. He was very tired from his journey, so we only stayed about ten minutes. We went to Mr. C.'s room and stables, and then visited the room of one of the Ensigns, Bowlby, who gave us a weak punch. (In a similar letter to his brother the 'punch' becomes 'whiskey'). *I went back to the Hotel at about eleven and had a bed there.*

I breakfasted next morning with Mr. C. who took me to the Quartermaster after breakfast. He appointed me a room. Mr. C. got me a servant and sent down some men to the Hotel for my luggage. I was very busy all day seeing my bed put up, and putting all my things to rights. At seven I put on my regimentals and went to Mess, where we had a capital dinner, and nearly all the officers took wine with me, but I took care not to take too much. They expect you to take wine on Wednesday, which is the strangers' day, but you need not on any other day, without you like. Will you ask Uncle John how I am to manage if anyone asks me to take wine, ask him how he did, and let me know when you write.

I shall not be drilled this week. They say I had better get a pair of the men's trousers and one of their jackets, which cost 8/-, to be drilled in, as it spoils the others. I shall want some carpet and muslin blinds. Please tell Mrs. Carey that I am much obliged to her for the letter to Mr. Carter, whom I like very much. Please excuse this note as the only pens I can find are dreadfully bad, and I have no knife to mend them."

Harry's uncle, John Loft, had served briefly with the 15th Hussars. He went on half-pay as a Lieutenant in 1819, and remained on half-pay until his death in 1873, still a Lieutenant. He was always most punctilious in matters of decorum and etiquette. Even when he was over seventy, and suffering badly from gout, he always rose from his chair when a lady entered the room, even if it was only his six-year-old great-niece. In reply to Harry's request, Uncle John wrote with high-minded advice.

10th July 1846

"I congratulate you on getting the worst over, that is the uncomfortable business of joining your Regiment, a stranger to everybody and everything. Give your best attention to learning your duty as an officer, because shortly you will be called upon to put the men through some manoeuvres, and how humiliating your situation if you neither know what words of command to give, nor whether they are properly obeyed. To be an efficient officer will gain you the favour off your Commanding Officer, which is very desirable, if it is honourably obtained. To be at all times neat and punctual, and making your duty be always your first consideration, will gain you the respect of your brother officers. With regard to taking wine on a day when you are required to take it, you will of course say 'With much pleasure' or 'I shall be very happy', - but on other days you should say 'Will you excuse me, I do not take wine today', as I think you will be better without it; but you will see what others do, and when you know the party better you will feel less uncomfortable at refusing, but I should say take it as seldom as possible, it is an expensive and growing evil, and you do not require it. I am glad the 64th is a cricketing regiment. Nothing will help you to feel at home more quickly."

Harry replied:

14th July 1846

"I am much obliged to you for getting me the nice carpet and blinds, and also to my Godmother for helping you to make them. (Margaret's response to Harry's remark, in his letter of 1st July, about the furnishings he needed for his room had been extremely prompt). *I breakfasted with Colonel Stretton and Mr. Carter this morning. The Colonel is a very nice person, and is very well liked indeed. He has seen a great deal of service. He was wounded by two musket balls at Vitoria* (The Duke of Wellington's defeat of the French in 1813) *and one of them is still in his side and pains*

him a good deal. We had a capital breakfast; bacon and eggs, cold ham, and marmalade. I should have gone with the rest to Church this morning, but Shotter has not sent me a tuft for my chaco, so I shall go to the Cathedral at three. I took a walk with Du Cane in the Duke of Ormond's grounds. What a beautiful castle it is! Do you remember it? I reckon so much on going about with you to see all the places, when you come. The Band plays there every Tuesday, so we get off the four o'clock drill. All the officers expect us to go abroad in about a year and a half.

Bowlby joined last Christmas and is now fourth on the Ensigns' List. The junior Ensign is called Thomson, but he has only just been gazetted, and does not join for two months. My baggage cost £3.13.0 coming to Ireland, which I paid yesterday and also a donation of 1/6d to the School. Du Cane had his baggage sent via Cork and it cost him £5.

On Wednesday night I slept in my own bed, and yesterday morning I breakfasted in the Mess, and at 2 pm. I had an hour's drill, and again at 4. In the evening I put on my red jacket, black trowsers (Harry's invariable spelling) *and sash (swords are not worn at dinner) and went to Mess. We had a capital dinner, the Colonel and most of the officers took wine with me, but I took care not to drink too much. We sat talking a long time, as it was the night guests are invited, and they expect you to take wine on that night.*

The next day I had an hour's drilling at 2 and another hour at 4. After breakfast I had only eaten some of those biscuits my Godmother was so kind as to give me, until dinnertime, when as soon as I had some soup I began to feel very sick and was obliged to leave the room. I was very sick when I got to my room, so I took some milk and went directly to bed. I was quite well this morning, and was up drilling at half past six till eight. I then had my breakfast in my room, and was again drilled from eleven to twelve, and from two to three, and again from four to five. I shall have this every day except Saturday, on which day we are only drilled from six to half past seven, for about three months, and glad I shall be when it is over.

My servant's name is Kenny; he seems a very decent fellow. I am to give him 2/- a week. His wife is to wash for me, for 10/- a month. Is that too much? I shall have to get him a suit of fustian and a livery, blue edged with red, which will cost £5. All the servants wear the same when they wait in the Mess. They take it in turns, about a week at a time. There are always 9 of them waiting. I do not know if I shall be able to keep him, as he is in Captain Yelverton's Company. He only gets back today, and I need his permission. I am in the Third, Captain James's, Company, who are on detachment.

I have been to the Cathedral. What a fine old building it is! There are a great many old memorials. Do you remember the one to Sir Dennis Pack? (As a General he ordered the 92nd into their famous charge at Waterloo and had been wounded in the battle.) *We had a very good sermon, delivered to a very poor congregation."*

8th July 1846

"I did not go to the Cathedral in my uniform. The Colonel and Major Duberly and Mr. Carter all went in plain clothes. The officers never wear their blue surtouts except on Parade and when on duty. I have never had mine on except the morning when I breakfasted with the Colonel, and I should not have had it on then, had it not been the first time. Singleton and Du Cane are being drilled now. Singleton has been at it for nearly three months. He is a nice sort of fellow, but terribly conceited. I like Bowlby very well. I have had my breakfast and tea with him, and today I had some potatoes and milk with him for luncheon. I hope I may be able to catch up with Du Cane. The men's trowsers I wear for drilling, I can wear afterwards, and the jacket I can most likely sell to one of the other Ensigns. Singleton's had been worn by 5 other Ensigns before he got it. Today I have been swinging clubs, facing about, and doing the balance step, and the positions for sword exercise, exactly the same as we used to do at Campbell's. The most difficult part I find is to lean forward and keep my body in, and my back straight.

Carter says the books I have are very good ones, particularly the one on Courts Martial. I have not written my name in them yet. I should like you to do it when you come, which I reckon of very much. I have had to pay 20 days pay towards the Mess, and also £1.5. 0. for public dinners which were given before I joined but after I had been appointed. We have to pay 2/4d. for our dinners, and on Wednesday you have to pay for wine, whether you drink it or not. Our dinners are very good, but no dessert; the pastry is very rich but not very substantial. I have not had to carve yet. The Colours are carried by the two Senior Ensigns. I shall have to pay £1 the first time I carry one, and another pound the first time I am on duty, and £2 to the Drill Sergeant when my drilling is over. I went down to the town yesterday to listen to the band. I think it is a pretty good one. There were a great many people to hear it.

Give my best love to my Godmother, and tell her I am much obliged to her for her advice about the Ham, and I will pay attention to it.

13th July 1846

"I have just posted a letter to Uncle Wallis. I told the man that the postage was only 5d. but after a deal of botheration he showed me in the book that it was 10d, so I had to pay it. I was silly enough to draw a sword in the anteroom on Friday for which I had to fork out a bottle of champagne. Nearly everyone in the Regiment has done it, but I knew nothing about it. (This sounds very much like a trick played on new members to the Mess) *There was a man flogged on Saturday for striking a Corporal. He had 150 lashes but he did not seem to care about it at all. Everyone has to be present, so I had no drilling. We had a game of cricket in the afternoon.* (It is impossible to say whether Harry was no more affected by the flogging than by the game of cricket, or whether he preferred not to dwell on it).

The other night Captain Parker bet Du Cane, who has been drilling for seven weeks today, that I am dismissed first. I shall do by best to win the bet for him. It is exactly three years last Friday since Lieut. Jopp and the first battalion of the 64th returned from Halifax, and, during the voyage home, ran against a rock. They expected the vessel would go down any minute and threw nearly all the officers' baggage overboard, and at length with great difficulty arrived at Goose Island, where they got the ship put to rights again. The men who were there kept the anniversary, and a great many of them got tipsy. Jopp says that he does not mind where the Regiment goes, as long as it is not Australia - 'anywhere but there'."

This refers to the adventures of two companies of the 64th who were returning to England after service in Newfoundland. Their ship, *The Alert*, struck a rock and was badly damaged. The Captain decided to run the ship ashore, and in order to maintain its equilibrium during this risky manoeuvre the troops lined up on the lower deck, where they remained until the danger was passed. Obviously they would have had little chance of escape if the ship had sunk. The water eventually reached their knees. Goose Island was uninhabited, so they had to live in shelters built from the wreckage until a relief ship was sent from Halifax. A General Order was subsequently issued ordering that the account of the detachment's discipline and courage should be read to every Regiment in the Army.

In 1852 there was a similar event when *The Birkenhead* was wrecked off the African coast. There were only 147 places in the lifeboats, so, while the women and children were being rescued, a large number of troops from several regiments were drawn up in line on the deck and remained there as the ship went down. In his poem "Soldier and Sailor Too" Kipling wrote in glowing terms of "The Birkenhead Drill". The 64th had been the first to carry out that drill.

Harry had been looking forward, or 'reckoning' as he called it, to a visit from Uncle Fred. Harry was able to announce his uncle's arrival to Margaret who was still staying with Mrs Carey at Carlow.

18th July 1846

"I was very much pleased on Wednesday to receive a note from Uncle saying he had just arrived, but not feeling very well after his journey. For the time he is staying at the same hotel as I stayed at, and we have been looking for lodgings for him, but have not been able to come up with any that Uncle likes very much and that are available immediately. He dined with us yesterday, when we had a very small party, but I think he liked it. He is also going to dine with us tonight, as one of the other officers has invited him. We have had two more games of cricket - one pretty good, and one moderate.

Bowlby was coming home from a party the other night in the back seat of the Colonel's carriage, when someone threw a great stone at him, and hit him on the shoulder. It hurt him very much at the time, and he suffered a great deal all through the night."

This is the first mention of the possibility of violence directed against the army or the authorities. Harry had so far made no reference to the blight that was wreaking havoc with the potato crop, and was to have so many repercussions upon the history of Ireland. He did acknowledge that the southeast of the island was much less affected by the blight than the west.

It seems that Fred had planned quite a long stay in Kilkenny. He soon found some lodgings to his liking, and was a frequent guest for dinner in the Mess, where he insisted on paying for himself. It had been arranged that Margaret should come to Kilkenny to see Harry and Uncle Fred. It seems that after her visit, they both went back to Carlow with her, staying there for at least one night.

8th August 1846

"I hope you are better now than when we left you this morning, and that you have not had one of your bad headaches as you were afraid you were going to have. Uncle and I arrived at Cowper Hill at a quarter to eight, and found Mr. Carter in a great fuss, as we had not got time to get to Kilkenny by a quarter past ten, and if he was not there by that time, he would be absent without leave, and be rowed by the Colonel, and would not be able to get leave next Tuesday, when he wants to go to a ball at Cowper Hill. We made all the haste we could, but Carter told me I should have to make my own excuses to the Colonel, but we agreed that Uncle was to see him, and make what excuses he could for both of us. We changed our car at Castle Comer, and arrived at Kilkenny at half past ten, and found to our great pleasure that the Colonel had been away since yesterday, and we had no trouble about it. It was a

beautiful drive up by Cowper Hill; I like a car much better than the inside of a coach"

The car Harry mentions was the Irish jaunting car, in which the passengers sit back to back, facing outwards, rather than forwards as in most horse-drawn vehicles. By 8th August Margaret was back in Louth. She had started her journey with £16 in her purse, and according to her accounts the whole journey cost £13.18, so she was puzzled to find that on her return home she still had £2.8.4, *"being 5/4d. more than I ought to have. This is very strange".*

Irish jaunting car.

Meanwhile Jem, Harry's brother, had been staying at Healing while their mother was in Ireland. Harry wrote to him for news from there:

15th July 1846

As I have nothing to do today I shall take a long walk by myself. I often think of you all at Healing, and wish I were there. Give my best love to them all, and say I shall be so glad to hear from any of them whenever they can find time to write. You can tell them this is a very sporting country, quite the Melton Mowbray of Ireland. Tell Uncle William that old Cure-all is well known even in this barbarous place. A troop of cavalry came up to exercise in the Barracks yesterday, but I never saw them prove distance to the left! (Uncle John as a half-pay officer in the Hussars, and Uncle William, who had been in the Lincolnshire Yeomanry, had possibly tried to teach Harry and Jem cavalry drill at Healing). *Mr. Carter told me this morning that he would get me on with my drill, and soon make me d - smart. He is a very nice person, and has been very kind to me.*

I should think you have been enjoying yourself very much, but I hope you look at your books sometimes. How are Crisp and Kitty? You must write me a long letter as soon as ever you can, and tell me how you all are, and how the crops and horses are, and every thing that is going on. Remember me to Mr. and Mrs. Wright, and

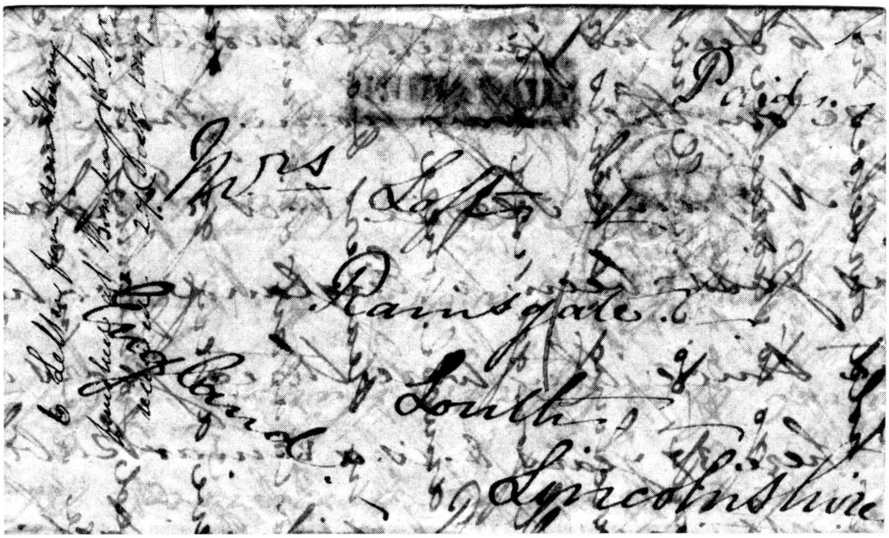

One of Harry's letters.

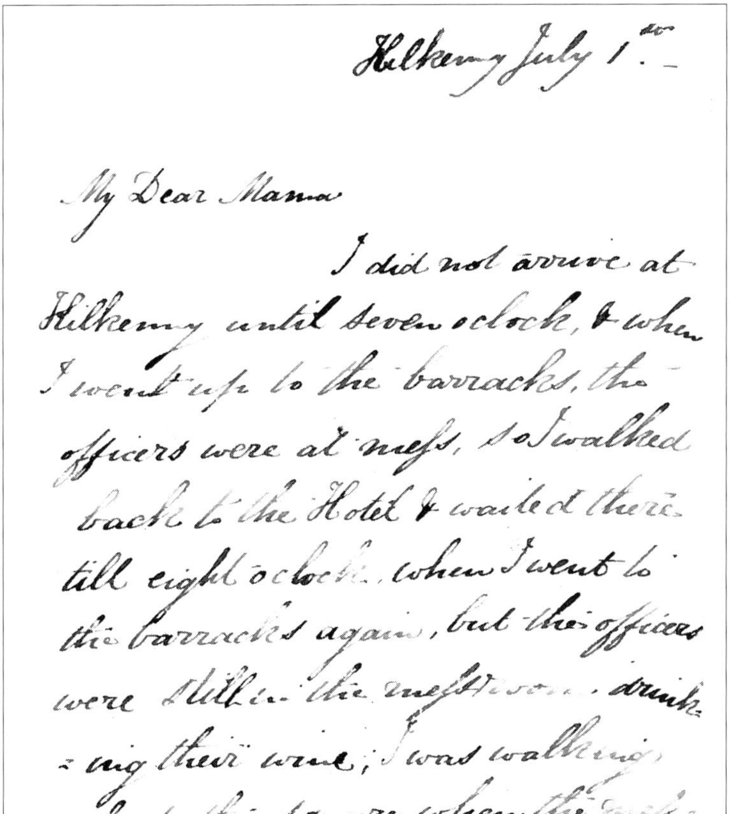
Kilkenny July 1st

My Dear Mama

I did not arrive at Kilkenny until seven oclock, & when I went up to the barracks, the officers were at mess, so I walked back to the Hotel & waited there till eight oclock, when I went to the barracks again, but the officers were still in the messroom, drink=ing their wine; I was walking about the square when the mess-waiter came running up to me & asked me if my name was Loft & told me that Mr Carter

Mr. and Mrs. Mason, and the Holgates, and tell them I would have called to see them, but had so little time. Give my love to them all at Grimsby, and tell me how the docks are going on. Give my love to Uncle Henry and Miss Holgate, and ask him to write when he can. I heard from Mama today. She is very well. You cannot think how pleased I was to receive her note. How is Aunt Lucy? Give her my love. Were there many mice in the stacks? I shall write again soon.

Your affectionate brother, J.H.C.Loft."

Grimsby had been little more than a village. It was a tidal port, which ships could enter or leave only at high tide. The first enclosed dock, that would make Grimsby into a port which ships could use at any state of the tide, was under construction. Together with the arrival of the railway, this brought about Grimsby's rapid growth into a large town with an increasing trade, especially for imports from the Baltic.

The construction of Grimsby Docks 1846-1852.

Crisp was the groom at Healing, who had been a great ally of the boys. His first name was Kitty, and he insisted that this really was his name, since it was given him at his baptism by a parson who was drunk at the time. He was very cross when he appeared in the 1841 Census as Christopher. The confusion was increased when he married a girl called Kitty!

Margaret always wrote, with a quill, a very regular and clear copperplate hand, which she had learned at Mr Scotts's Academy in Edinburgh, and for which she had won numerous prizes. So her letters were, and remain, easily legible, even though she usually crossed her letters by writing down the page vertically, and then writing across the page horizontally. This was a common practice at the time, and ensured that she got twice as much news on the paper, and so paid only the minimum postage. Very occasionally she even wrote diagonally as well! Every week Harry received a long letter from his mother, who was a tireless correspondent. *"What a nice long letter you wrote to me. I can read the crossing very well, and instead of being tired, as you say, I was very sorry when it was finished, and I hope you will write them quite as long, when you have time."*

Harry's writing, also with a quill, was almost as regular and legible as his mother's. Originally he always started *"My Dear Mama",* which later became *"My Dear Mother",* and concluded *"Believe me ever, my dear Mama, your most affectionate Son, J.H.C. Loft".* He sealed the envelopes with sealing wax and a signet ring, given to him by his uncle James Wallis Loft. The crest on it was a hand holding a dagger, which was the crest on the coat of arms used by General John Henry Loft, although he had never received a grant of arms and so had no right to use one. Coincidentally, Margaret's father in Edinburgh also used a coat of arms to which he was not entitled.

Harry often received a letter from his brother as well, which was almost as good, especially if it had news from Healing in it. Sometimes James illustrated his letters with drawings, for Harry wrote to say how much he liked the drawing of a splendid

Healing Church

The Reverend James Edmund Wallis Loft, Harry's brother Jem, when he was Rector of Healing.

race course, with Repealer (one of Uncle Fred's steeplechasers) winning a most desperate race. He also exchanged letters with his friends at Louth Grammar Sc hool, particularly Charley Banks, the son of Dr John Banks, and Faulkner (Faulky) Allison. Uncle Fred was a fairly regular correspondent, and Harry occasionally wrote to some of the other Loft uncles. He usually wrote to Louth every Sunday, and like his mother often 'crossed' his letters. The letters to and from Louth usually took three, occasionally four, days to reach their destination.

13th August 1846

"Thompson joined yesterday so I am no longer Junior. I have been president this week, and have got on pretty well with the carving so far. Uncle has been very poorly since we were at Carlow with you. He has scarcely been out of the house all that time."

29th August 1846

"I was never so surprised in all my life as when I saw Uncle William walk into my room last Friday. On the spur of the moment he sailed from Liverpool in the morning by the mail packet, and stayed the night in Dublin. He never told anybody he was going. He was not much troubled with luggage. The only thing he brought was a brush, and he left that in Dublin. (Uncle Fred was something of a dandy, while William was notorious for his casual ways and dress, but he seems to have been just as acceptable a Mess guest as his brother.) *He asked about, and noticed, everything, sheep, horses, crops, land, castles, and I think in the short time he was here he got to know more than many people would learn in a month. He thought the people were a queer set, and said he should take a deal of persuading to live here.*

I began the Light Company drill yesterday, but I shall not get it over before the three months. Uncle Fred is not much better. He says his head is so bad that he cannot write to you, but I am sure that he will as soon as he can. He is on the sofa nearly all the day".

5th September 1846

"I am at the saluting and at the officer's part of the drill now, and am very hoarse with shouting to the men. I hope I shall be dismissed by the end of this month. Do you think my seal is large enough, and should I use red or black wax with it?"

13th September

"I am sorry to say that Uncle is much worse. He has had attacks of intermittent fever, and has been in bed for the last three days, and has taken scarcely anything but gruel and tea. He is looking very ill and thin, but the Doctor thinks him better today. The Doctor says it is not at all infectious, so you need not be afraid, Dear Mama, of my taking it. I am much obliged to you for telling me of those words which I spell

Kilkenny Cathedral, where Harry met a Canon who had known Harry's father, Thomas Loft, when he was serving with the Gordon Highlanders there, 14 years previously.

The Castle and River Barrow at Kilkenny.

wrong, but the thing is, I seldom have time to look over my letters to you.

I have not seen much of James, my Captain, yet, but from what I have seen of him I think I shall like him very well. The Lieutenant of my Company is called Burne, but I do not know anything about him. I do not think there is any chance of my changing my rooms for better ones, as you suggest. In fact there is an advantage in not having good rooms, since if a Captain comes and wants a room, he can turn any Sub out and take his room. This happened last week when Capt. Errington came in from detachment and turned Singleton out of his room, because it was a very good one. My servant is called Murphy. He has not been a servant before, but he does very well, and he used to be a groom, so we can talk about horses. If he behaves himself I shall most likely keep him as long as we are both in the Regiment. The clothes and shoes fit him, and he looks very well in his livery when he is waiting at the Mess - quite the smartest in the Regiment. They cannot find any potatoes here, and are beginning to complain of the turnips, and the Indian meal is running very low, so that they hardly know how they are to get through the winter."

Indian meal, maize, had been imported to Ireland to take the place of the diseased potatoes. It was unfamiliar, and not very acceptable, to the Irish peasants, but was the only substitute available in large quantities.

A contemporary engraving of the Irish Famine.

Harry's servant, George Murphy, is the only Private whom Harry mentioned in his letters. A Catholic, he had joined the Regiment in Dublin in 1839, aged 19, when he was described as a Labourer. At 5' 8½" he was taller than most of the other Privates in Harry's Company, and had been awarded one Good Conduct Medal, so he may well have been particularly smartly turned out as a Mess Waiter. He was a married man, with one child, a daughter. Since he had married after obtaining permission from the Colonel, his wife was entitled to accompany him when on detachment and to share his accommodation in barracks. Although their backgrounds and their ages were very different Harry and Murphy seem to have established a real friendship over the next three years, partly through their shared interest in horses and steeple chasing, and to have parted with genuine regret in 1849, when Harry went abroad and Murphy remained in England.

20th September 1846

"Uncle is still very ill in bed; he is very weak and in bad spirits. The Doctor thinks he is rather better and going on well, and is out of danger, but does not expect to see any great change in him until after tomorrow, which will be the 14th day of the fever. I have had to write some letters for him about some shares, and to Uncle William about things at Healing. He bid me tell Uncle W. that he never felt worse in his life, or more like dying; that the Doctor gave him every hope, but he did not know what there was to hope for. I do not like to hear him talking this way, but he fancies himself worse than he really is.

The Doctor and an apothecary have been calling twice a day. I have often to speak to Uncle five or six times before he answers me, and sometimes he hardly knows what he is saying. He can eat nothing but jelly, arrowroot with wine in it, beef tea and those kinds of thing. I am with him as much as I can, and the people in the house are very kind; Bessie is always with him when I am away. They have had some bark put down in the street. (This was sometimes done in order to lessen the noise from the hooves and wheels of horse-drawn vehicles, which might have disturbed the rest of a seriously ill patient.) *I have to attend Parade now, as I am getting close to being dismissed. My old common shirts are beginning to wear a little. Do you think I could have them fronted, when I have finished drilling, and would they be able to do it here? I heard from the War Office on Sunday, telling me that my application for exemption from Income Tax has been allowed. so that I can claim back what has been deducted from my pay. My pay is lasting very well. Uncle does not yet feel himself strong enough to read your letter, but thinks in a day or two he should be able to make one out. He was very pleased when I read your last letter to him. Last week I wrote to Uncle William, to you and Jem, to Jim Iles, to Aunt Christina, to Lizzie Lundie, to Henry Iles, and to the Army agent. I think I have done very well."*

29th September 1846

"I am very happy to inform you that poor Uncle is much better. The fever has entirely left him, and there is nothing the matter with him now, but debility. The Doctor only comes once a day. He says the only thing Uncle has to do now is to get as strong as possible as fast as he can, and that he has made a good fight of it. He got

up for the first time yesterday and sat out for about an hour, though I had to help him across the room. The people in the house have been very kind indeed. Bessie sat with him nearly every night."

Uncle Fred's condition continued to improve and there was good news for Harry in another way.

6th October 1846

"Last Tuesday Carter dismissed Du Cane, and I was dismissed on Thursday, so that I have only had three months and three days of it. Singleton joined in January and is at drill now. I am supernumerary on duty today. Uncle Fred is better some days than others. His appetite is at last very good. He was going for a drive in an outside car today, but I have not seen him as I am on duty. The Doctor has discontinued his visits for more than a week now."

We had two officers of the Scots Greys to dine with us last night, as they were passing through on detachment. I saw the Troop come in; they are very fine fellows indeed. The Cornet has 17 horses of his own! They have to march in full dress, which I should think the officers do not much like. They expected there would be a row here on Friday, so we were all confined to barracks, but there was not anything to do, and they have been very quiet since, and nearly all the poor people about here have been employed, with 1/6d a day wages. It is thought there will be no general leave this year, on account of the disturbed state of the country.

We began to wear our winter black trousers on Saturday, which is rather a bother, as I have two pairs of blue ones, which I have never had on, and the other pair is as good as new, and I should think they will be rather small for me by next year. Shotter had no business to sell me so many pairs. We now get two boxes of coal a week instead of one, and four candles a week. We dine at 7 o'clock and shall do so all the winter. Captain Norris has got an appointment as Surveyor of Roads somewhere, and is off all regimental duty. It is a capital thing for him, as he will have a guinea a day and all his expenses paid.

Murphy broke my nice washbasin the other day. I do not know what part of the country he comes from. He is a regular Irishman but I like him very much. He does not speak a word of Irish. He waits at table very well, and he has everything very comfortable for me."

13th October 1846

"Uncle is gaining strength very fast, though he does not yet look very stout or red-faced. He was weighed the other day and has lost one and a half stones, since we were all weighed at Waithe Mill. (Waithe Mill was close to Uncle Fred's stables at Grainsby). I *was horrified when I got on the scales to find that I weighed 11 stone 8 pounds, which I think is dreadful. I was also measured by the stand with which they*

measure the soldiers, and discovered I measured 5ft 11in. in my socks. I do not think there is anyone here who takes likenesses, but I will get you one as soon as I can.

It was very kind of Mr. J. Emeris to write to Mr. Drapes about me. He left a card with the Sergeant Major and said he would like to see me, so I called there yesterday. They lost a little girl the day they got Mr. Emeris's letter, so they are going into the country for a short time, but said they would be happy to see me when they come back. They live near the Cathedral and he does duty there. They have two or three other children.

22nd October 1846

"Uncle is going on capitally, and getting quite strong. We had a long walk this morning, and he did not seem at all tired. He looks much better tho' still very thin. We were weighed again today. He only weighs 10st. 6lb. but I weigh 11st. 11lb. - 3 pounds more than last time! I only weighed 10st. 10lb. when I left Louth. I think Uncle will not go to Healing after all. The Doctor advises him to go to some warmer place in the south of England, so I should think he will go to Bath.

The Circus is here and was under our patronage last Monday night. The Colonel and nearly all the officers went, but I could not as I was on duty. I had to sign 140 passes for men who wanted to go to the Circus. I am told there were about 500 people present altogether.

We are to be inspected by General Wyndham next Tuesday and we are busy preparing for it. I was sorry to hear that all the Healing, horses, even old Cure-all, have had distemper very badly, so they will not be able to have much hunting before Christmas.

One of the officers of the Scotch Greys, Sir George Handson, is a very consequential fellow, and gave himself a great many airs to one of our Captains. They are now on detachment at the same place, and as Sir George is only a Lieutenant, it will be rather awkward for him, as he cannot get a day's leave without asking the Captain for it.

31st October 1846

"The Inspection was a splendid day. I think we looked very well. The General came up about 11 am. when we were formed into line, and he inspected each man, and we then marched past three or four times. He generally calls out some of the officers to drill the Regiment, but he was in a hurry, as he had to visit all our detachments. The two senior Ensigns generally carry the Colours, but for some reason or other Thompson and I had the pleasure. The flag staffs are 12 feet long, and the Colours six feet square, but we had belts and there was not a breath of wind, so we had no difficulty in carrying them. The belt went over my epaulette and I was afraid it might injure it, but it did not do so. I carried the Queen's Colour.

The General dined with us on Monday, when we had a very grand dinner, with 23 sitting down, and 16 wax candles on the table. These public dinners have been rather expensive, but I have some money left, and I don't suppose there will be any more this winter. We all had our coatees buttoned up, and kept our swords on during dinner. (They usually dined with their coatees open, over a white waistcoat). *Uncle saw the Inspection so will be able to give you an account of it.*

We went route-marching on Thursday. Uncle came up for the parade, and marched with us. He was rather tired, but as the band played nearly all the way he liked it very well. It was only about four miles, as it was the first time, but we shall go out twice a week until April, and will soon have good long marches.

Uncle left yesterday morning on the coach. I was on duty but managed to get down to Mrs. Guilfoile's just as he was leaving, and I rode about a mile on the box with him, and then walked home to my breakfast, which I did not enjoy very much! It has been very nice for me having him here, and I miss him very much already.

I hope to get another step soon, as one of our Lieutenants is going to sell out. I have my fire kept in all day now. My washerwoman airs my things well, but I always do it before I put them on. Thank you, dear Mama, for getting me the muffattees. I really cannot think who the young lady is that knitted them, without it is Miss Daniel. (Muffattees were some kind of mitten. In fact it was Ann Cropper who had knitted them.)

This illustration of a soldier of the 98th Regiment of Foot (North Staffordshire), in the 1840s, probably reflects the appearance of Harry's soldiers.

Courtesy of Rob Chapman, Flintlock Publishing.

Give my best love to Faulk. I was so sorry to hear about his poor mother's death, and pity him and his brothers very much."

Although Harry was sorry to lose his uncle's company, it must have been also something of a relief to him, since he had been acting as his secretary, writing letters to his bankers about his investments, and to William Loft about the management of affairs at Healing. Margaret had obviously been showing maternal concern for Harry's welfare, in addition to worrying about the state of his clothes.

11th November 1846

"There is no danger in my going walking by myself, and I would often much rather be on my own. I generally take a good long walk every day. Last Sunday, when I was out, I met a person called Shannon, a Canon in the Cathedral here, and he began talking to me about the 92nd. He surprised me by remembering that I was born in it. He knew my Father very well, and all the officers, as well as a lad could know men. He told me the names of all the Ensigns at that time, although he was only young then. He thinks they were Lockhart and Ormesby. He is a very nice fellow, and knows nearly everything about everybody. Do you remember him? He is quite young, I should think about 30 or 32. We had a pleasant walk together."

Harry did not remember his father, but he was always very proud of him, and of his connection with the 92nd.

In answer to this letter Margaret wrote:

"Archie Lockhart was the brother of John Lockhart, Sir Walter Scott's son-in-law. It was he who did the likeness of Donald Cameron Smith, who played the gallant 92nd into the charge at Waterloo. He was a great mimic and a most amusing fellow. I cannot remember Ormesby so well. He was a very little fellow."

Lieutenant Colonel Lockhart distinguished himself as commanding officer of the 92nd during the Indian Mutiny.

In his letters Harry often recalled what he and his mother and brother had been doing on the same date in the previous year, and wishing that they could be doing the same things together again; driving home from Healing, or going to dinner with friends, or walking in the Cow Pastures or on Fisher's Hill. Sometimes he wondered what they were doing at Louth as he wrote; sitting comfortably by the fire, as Jim did his schoolwork, or going for their regular Sunday afternoon walk. He described how he spent his day, now that he had been dismissed from drilling:

"I have my breakfast at 8.0 am, and afterwards learn some French until about 10.20 am, when I get ready for parade. After parade I go for a walk and learn some more French, or write my letters, until about 5.30 pm, when we get ready for dinner. Afterwards I read a book and some verses from the Bible. Du Cane has lent me a good one, The O'Donoghue by Charles Lever. Butter is only a shilling a pound, and eggs two for 1½d. I don't know anything about flour; the bread is 2d a pound. I have plenty of blankets and everything I want. My room is never very cold, because the door and the window are on the same side and there is no chimney. My thin unbleached nightshirt is full of holes in the back. Ought it have done so? Have I had

it long? I do not want poor Jim to write oftener than he likes, as I know he has not much time, but I reckon much on his letters. I now suspect that it was one of the Miss Iles who made my muffattees."

22nd November 1846

"I marched the Roman Catholics to their chapel this morning, and went to the Cathedral at noon. Godley joined on Thursday; a little fellow from Sligo. He will have a very disagreeable time for his drilling in the winter weather. They expect this will be a terrible winter, with the potatoes nearly all finished, and everything so dear. Friday was a Day of general humiliation and prayer to be observed all over Ireland. Was it the same in England? Captain Draper is on the Staff in Dublin, so his promotion will not do me any good. I see Major General Wyndham is made a Lieutenant General and is leaving Ireland, so he will not inspect us again. Also Colonel MacDonald is made a Major General, and a Macdonald appointed to the 92nd. Is he any relation? (Colonel MacDonald had commanded the 92nd in Thomas Loft's time with the Regiment.) *They were saying the other day that 20 officers have left our Regiment in the past three years. Singleton only joined 8 months ago, and he is now first for purchase. There is a rumour that 10,000 men are to be sent to Portugal. It would be nicer than going to India.*

29th November 1846

"We are having the first real winter weather, with quite a lot of snow, and a freezing wind. Before this it had been raining every day for a fortnight. We have only been able to get out route-marching twice, and have had no parades. Du Cane is going on detachment on Monday, for which I am sorry, as I think I like him the best of any body here. My washerwoman was married yesterday to a man in our Company, who has nearly served his time and will be discharged in about two months, so I shall have to get someone else. I think if Murphy's wife washes I shall have her. At present she is at the Dean's, nursing, where she has been for the past seven months. She mended my nightshirt last week. I have been obliged to have my surtout let out; Murphy thinks it will do for the next two months! I tried on a pair of black regimental trousers the other day, which I have never worn yet, and I could not make them meet, and they were a deal too short. The tailor says they will let out enough. I have no chilblains, and I do not suffer at all from cold feet.

I like being Orderly Officer very well, tho' it is a bit bothering not to be able to get out of barracks. It was the fair here yesterday; very much like the Louth Status. I am sorry I could not get you and Jim a fairing. Either Bickerstaff or Burne is likely to get the Adjutancy when Carter goes. He does not have anything to do with it. The Colonel chooses whom he likes. There is no chance of my getting it. Carter expects to get his Company in a year's time, and you must be two years in the Regiment before you can be Adjutant. The officers are all in good health, except for Shute, who has just got his lieutenancy, but has been on sick leave for two months and has just got two more. I have been out shooting with Thompson and Du Cane. Singleton gave me a snipe the other day, and I had it for my breakfast. Murphy and I think we cooked it pretty well.

6th December 1846

"At 3 am yesterday a magistrate came here for some soldiers, as there was a row in the town. The Colonel sent Captain Parker and Bowlby with 60 men, and as I was on duty I had to go with them. There was a great mob near the Cathedral who had attacked a baker's shop and broken every pane of glass in the house. We marched down into the middle of them, and then faced right and marched on to the pavement, and stood with our backs against the houses opposite the shop. When the soldiers marched at them, the people scattered, and there was a great pushing and scrambling to get out of our way.

We stayed some time, while the people were calling us names all the time, and telling us how useless we were. Some policemen were left in the house, and we went off towards the barracks. The people thought we were going away, but we turned to the right into High Street, and caught some fellows breaking into another baker's shop. When we came up they rushed out, but the magistrate jumped off his horse and seized two of them, and Parker and Bowlby caught two more, who pulled them into the crowd and they had a regular scuffle, but they got all four of them.

We then went to the market house, where we stayed and went up the stairs. The people followed us to the door, shouting and making a dreadful noise. The soldiers were put in the Ballroom, and we were in the Council room. The magistrates had a meeting, but I do not think they knew what to do, as they had no work for the people. The Mayor ordered some dinner to be sent to us. The people attacked two other shops, but the police dealt with them, and three mounted police were patrolling the streets all the time, so we were not called out again, and as everything was quiet by 9 pm we came home. The police are useless without they have us to back them, and the people hate them very much.

The Relief Committee was to meet today to see what can be done for the people, as if nothing is done soon there will be a regular row. One of the magistrates said he heard a countryman say to a townsman last night, 'You are fine talkers, but if you were to turn out like men you would have all the boys in the county in to help you.' They have all been employed, but they have nothing for them to do now. They can all have one meal a day at the poor house, but that is not enough."

9th December 1846

"The town is now quiet again. The magistrates were expecting more trouble, so we always have 60 men ready to turn out at a moment's notice. They have employed 20 people and those who are not can still have a meal at the poor house, but they cannot live upon that, and many of them have nothing else. The detachments will be relieved at the end of the month, but I do not know whether I shall go or not, as the Colonel does not often send young officers. The senior Captain has his choice of places, and I think James will go to Castlecomer. I should like to go with them. It would be a change."

13th December 1846

"The wintery weather continues, and I hope we shall have some good skating tomorrow, as there has been no snow to spoil the ice. I put on my thick flannel shirts and drawers today, and find them very warm and comfortable. The muffattees are very useful now. The town remains very quiet. A great many more people have been employed, and they are going to make a great quantity of soup, and sell it to the people at 1d. a quart. as they say the people would not thank them for it, if it was free. They are going to cut a drain from the Barracks to the river, which will employ 300 men. I heard that the ringleaders last Saturday were all men who had employment, and were well off. Do you remember that it is just a year ago since we sat in our own seat in church for the first time?"

21st December 1846

"Last week I had to attend two Courts Martial, as a supernumerary, to learn what is done. We had some skating but now it is getting milder, and the rain has come back, so the town is dreadfully dirty. There has not been the slightest disturbance in the town. They are employing many more men, but they have cut up that road out by the Jesuits' College, that was the only good road out of town, but they have to find them employment of some sort. We are sending out a detachment to Tulloch, a village near Carlow, where there are some very large mills, which might be attacked.

I have often thought of you this last week, and wished I could be with you spending Christmas at Barnoldby, like we did in 1843. Give the Iles my best love. I used always to enjoy Christmas so much, especially when we went to Healing, but I do not reckon of it at all this year. I am sure you will enjoy yourselves. Do you remember the last time we went to Healing in the cart, and we were so cold when we got there, and Grandmama had that fine chicken pie ready for us? Do you remember that last Christmas we sat in our own seat in church for the first time? I can remember the text Dr. Badcock preached from."

27th December 1846

"I marched the Roman Catholics to Chapel this morning, and the Priest gave out that the Bishop had been pleased to allow the indigent poor to receive soup on Fridays as well as on other days. I pity the poor wretches being obliged to ask the Bishop's leave to eat when they are actually starving. I was on duty on Christmas Day, a beautiful clear frosty day. I marched the men to Church in the morning, and afterwards we all went round the men's dinners with the Colonel. The officers always give a sovereign each to their Companies, and they subscribe so much themselves, and have a regular feast, with ale and wine. In every room they gave the Colonel a drink and he wished them a Merry Christmas. My Company was the only one which did not have a special dinner, as they owe a great deal of money at Carrick where they were on detachment, so Captain James is going to pay it off, instead of giving them anything. Everyone had a regular merry afternoon, and a great many of them got tipsy, but that is overlooked on Christmas Day as long as they keep quiet, as it is the only day in the year they have to themselves.

I did not much enjoy Christmas. It is the first one I have spent without any of my relations. We had a very small party at Mess; there were only four of us and a Lieutenant in the Engineers, who is quartered here, but we had a very good dinner. Roast beef, Turkey and Plum Pudding were the principal dishes. After dinner we sat round the fire, but at 8.30 pm I had to see that all the men were in Barracks, as I was still on duty.

4th January 1847

On New Year's Day there was a slight row here; they attacked some bakers' shops, but the police were able to put a stop to it, without requiring our assistance. There was a disturbance too at the Poor House. I think they will be unable to give the people dinners there any longer. There has been a subscription in the town, and our Officers have given £17. There was a sermon about it on Sunday.

There is a troop of the Queen's Bays here now and their Captain dined with us; he is a very funny-looking fellow. He has a great deal of hair, immense great curling mustachios and eyebrows and an imperial. When he laughs he shuts his eyes, so that his nose is the only part of his face that you can see. The military papers say a great deal about our all having to wear mustachoes but I do not know if this is true, but I hope not, since I do not shave much yet."

One of our Lieutenants, who was doing Captain's duty, has got an appointment on the staff of his uncle, General Napier, at Limerick, so my Lieutenant has taken the command of his Company. Our Company is going on detachment to Wexford next week, and I will be the only other officer apart from Capt. James, and as he is a married man I shall have the pleasure of being the whole Officers' Mess."

So Harry was to start another stage in his military experience.

Templemore

CHAPTER 4

ON DETACHMENT

There were always a considerable number of regiments stationed in Ireland, and it was the custom to move them from one garrison town to another fairly frequently, so that there was a constant movement of troops from place to place. Every regiment always had a number of companies, and sometimes even smaller units, scattered over a wide area, so as to have troops available wherever trouble might break out. Life on detachment was usually preferred to life in barracks, as it provided more freedom and fewer ceremonial duties.

In January 1847, Harry went on detachment for the first time. His account of the march to Wexford is typical of the many such marches he was to experience. His letters at this time contain various references to the state of Ireland during the potato famine, showing his feelings about some of the people involved. His views and prejudices were derived from his family background, his age and his upbringing in a small town. It would be unrealistic to expect him, a young man of sixteen, to give a balanced picture of a very complex political, social and economic state of affairs.

10th Jan. 1847

"My Dear Mama, You can readily fancy how anxiously I watched for the Corporal returning from the post this morning and how pleased I was to receive your nice long letter. Last Thursday I was very busy packing and had everything ready for weighing by 4 o'clock. (There was a limit to the amount of baggage an Officer could take with him, unless he was prepared to pay for it himself.) *I slept that night in Godley's room on some cushions with a horse-rug and a large Scotch plaid to cover me. We left Kilkenny at 8 am on Friday. The Band came a mile out of town with us, playing "The Girls we left behind us." It was a very fine day. As soon as we leave the town the men march as they like, and sing and smoke as long as they keep going. We reached Thomastown, 12 English miles away, at noon, which is not very quick work, but quite fast enough for the men. We had three breaks but only for five minutes. We were billeted in the hotel which was a very poor one. I had to be on parade at three o'clock to see that the men were all sober, and afterwards I took a long walk to Jerpoint Abbey, which has been a very large building indeed and is a very fine ruin, getting back in time for dinner at six o'clock.*

Next day after a 9am start we reached New Ross at 3 pm (16 miles). It is a nice place and there is a very good hotel. We have a subaltern's detachment there and there is also a troop of the Bays. We had a boiled turkey for dinner, and as we had had a long march we finished it entirely the next day, Sunday. We marched the men to church in the morning and in the afternoon we had a long walk, where we met a

Mr. Howlan, a great Horseman and a regular traveller who amused us very much. He travels for three or four months each year, and farms during the rest. He told us a great many wonderful stories.

Monday was a hard march; I marched with the men and James went by the car. We had a sixteen mile march to Taghmon which is a wretched little village. We were six hours on the march as it is all up and down hill, and the roads are very bad. They were lowering the road over one hill, and it was so bad that the baggage could not get that way and had to go on to Wexford, so that when we got to Taghmon I was wet through and could not change my things.

Next morning we only had nine miles to march, and reached Wexford at noon. This is a long straggling place with very narrow and dirty streets. The harbour is a very fine one indeed, but there is so much sand and mud in the middle of it that no large vessels can get in. The Barracks are rather small but very nice ones, from which we have a very good view of all the ships. James is at present in lodgings but he will move into Barracks as soon as he can get furniture. My rooms are very like the ones I had at Kilkenny. There are two rooms below mine, which I shall use as a kitchen, and let Murphy and his wife live in them. I have not seen Mrs. James yet, but I hear she is a very nice woman. They have only one child, about six months old.

We have parade every morning if it is fine. I go round the men's dinners at 1 pm, and turn out the guard once during the day and once at night, and visit the sentries but I can do this when I like. James will do it for me whenever I ask him. Altogether I think I shall like it here very much. Two or three people have called upon us, and last night we were invited to a party. James would not go, so I went by myself at about nine o'clock and danced away like a mad man till three o'clock this morning. It is the first one there has been here for some time. Stirling, who was here before us only went out once. There were about 28 people at the party; there would have been more if the bad weather had not prevented them. There was a capital supper. We finished with Sir Roger de Coverley, which I rather liked. We got home about 3am.

This is one of the quietest counties in Ireland but an agent, Capt. Hunt, was shot near here last Saturday night. He was returning to his home a few miles out of town in a car. His servant had just got off to open the garden gate, which they had fastened. As Hunt bent down to take the reins a man fired a blunderbuss at him, which was placed on a wall about a yard from the car. If it had been loaded with ball he must have been killed, but he had a great deal of clothing on so some of the shot glanced off; they found 18 in his clothes, but some entered his neck and shoulders. Everyone says he deserved it, and that he will be shot at again before long. He has just ejected two tenants who had never owed a shilling of rent in their lives."

Captain James was the only other officer with the Company, so Harry had to perform a Lieutenant's duty. It seems that he must sometimes have been rather lonely, though he was fortunate enough to find friends in the local community.

23rd January 1847

"I am very comfortable now and like being here very much. We have parade every morning when it is fine. At one o'clock I go round the men's dinners, and then get something to eat myself, turn out the guard, and then go out walking, sometimes with James, but generally by myself. I wear my blue surtout (an 'undress' frock coat, rather than the full-dress scarlet coatee) *a good deal now, as it is a bother changing so often. I was measured on my birthday, and am a little more than 6 feet in my boots.*

1st Feb. 1847

"On Sunday I march the Roman Catholics to their Chapel, which is a very fine one, with a large congregation, including a great many respectable people; and at 12 I go with the other men to Church. The Communion Table is on the North side, which I have not seen before. There is a Club here of which we are honorary members; they have all the papers and magazines there. I went to see if Uncle had again entered old Cure-all for the Liverpool this year. It is not half so expensive being here as at Headquarters. I have not shaved yet, but I expect I shall have to do so before very long. (This last point was of some concern to him, as there was a strong rumour that all Army officers would be required to wear a moustache!)

I am very comfortable now and get on very well. I like being here and never feel at all dull. We have been out route-marching for two hours this morning, instead of Friday, the usual day. It is bitterly cold and we have had some snow. Miss Heron or The Infant Power, whom perhaps you have heard of, is now here, and we shall probably be asked for our patronage. They were at Kilkenny and had our Band one night, but I did not go. When you see Mrs. Banks next please tell her there is not much fear of anyone falling in love with me, or I with anyone, but if such a thing should happen I will let her know."

Margaret had obviously conveyed a comment on Harry's social life from her friend Susan Banks, the wife of Dr Banks and mother of Harry's great friend Charley. In the whole of Harry's existing correspondence to his mother and brother there is no suggestion of any attachment to a girl. It may have been otherwise in his letters to his friends.

"Yesterday I had some roast beef for dinner, which Murphy cooked very well, and today I had boiled mutton and some broth. Instead of pudding I have bread and cheese, but when my kitchen is ready I must try to have some. It will be fine fun for me, teaching Murphy to cook them. James and his wife are in barracks now. They are both very glad to get out of the nasty dirty streets. My money gets on pretty well; I have some left. It is much less expensive living here than at Headquarters."

7th Feb. 1847

"I have been out shooting a few times with James, and I went to breakfast with

them on Thursday to help them to eat some of the snipe we had shot. I have dined with a Captain Kennedy of the Navy, who is the commander of the Coast Guard here. He has got the appointment, which I believe is worth £500 until they have a ship for him. He knew our Regiment in Jamaica. He is a married man but has left his wife in England. We had a barnacle, like a wild goose but not so large. It was the best bird I ever tasted. They come to feed in the harbor, which is nothing, but mud, and men go out at night with great guns and knock a great many of them over at one shot. This one was killed with 29 others at one shot. I intend to buy some when they are in the market. They are only 3/- a couple. After dinner we went to see The Infant Power, who is certainly a wonderful little girl but you see quite enough of her in one night. I have had a long letter from Uncle Fred, who says that old Cure is entered for the Liverpool Steeplechase and Repealer for the Hurdles. There are 60 horses entered for the Steeplechase which is the greatest number ever known. I hope they will be luckier with their racing than they were last year."

15th Feb.1847

"The weather is now rather warm. Last week it was freezing very hard. All the old people say this is the most severe winter there has been in Ireland for a long time. Here I am the President, Vice-president, and all the members of the Mess. My kitchen is now finished. Murphy and his wife live in it, and we get on very well. I had a rather curious dinner today - fried pork and boiled turnips. I did not really know how it would be, but Murphy was sure it would be very good, and I liked it very well, but you must not take this as a specimen of my dinners. I have beefsteaks, boiled beef, roast mutton, roast pork, and Murphy cooks it all capitally. We have some good potatoes at 1s.2d. a stone. The only thing I venture to have in the shape of a pudding is boiled rice as we used to have it. I have it boiled in water for above an hour, and then in milk for a short time. Murphy does it very nicely since I instructed him in the art. I had a barnacle the other day. Eggs are hard to get and dreadfully dear. I must see if Murphy's wife can make me any proper puddings. The shore here is nothing but mud."

Harry frequently dined with Captain and Mrs James, and enjoyed their company.

"They have only been married a little over a year. Mrs. James is a pretty little woman, and a very nice person indeed, with a beautiful voice. We all went to another party on Thursday with another capital supper, and plenty of music and dancing. Captain Kennedy was there in his uniform, which looks very well. He is a very amusing fellow - a regular sailor. I think he is an Irishman but am not quite sure. I called there next day. Ought I to have done so, or should I have waited a few days?"

Sometimes Harry and the Captain went out shooting together, and at other times Harry used to take the James's enormous Newfoundland dog, called Neptune, with him on his walks for company.

"He is black and white and would be very handsome if his tail and ears had not been cropped. He is the best-tempered dog I ever saw. He is a great favourite with the men." The weather did not bother Harry; *"With my oilskin cover on my cap, and my cloak, I do not care about anything. I go about 5 or 6 Irish miles every day."*

Harry continued to be invited out by local families: *"At the last party I danced nothing but Quadrilles, as none of the gentlemen would dance the Polka or the Celeries, and waltzing makes me dizzy. There were some nice girls there, in fact three or four very pretty ones. I did not go in my uniform."*

23rd Feb. 1847

"Yesterday I dined with the Jameses, to meet Captain Kennedy and a Mr. Redmond. We had a good deal of singing by Mrs. James and Mr. Redmond. I was right about Capt. Kennedy; he is an Irishman, but he has a very moderate opinion of his country, so we had plenty of arguing between him and Mr. Redmond, who is a red-hot Republican.

Do you remember Mr. Hunt who I told you had been shot at a short time ago? Capt. Kennedy met him yesterday in a tax-cart with a policeman with a loaded carbine on each side of him. He said he blushed for his country; he had been in almost every country in the world, but he had never heard of such a thing in his life. Mr. Hunt received a letter a short time since saying 'I missed you last time but I will have some better powder next time and I will kill you.' He showed this to the magistrates and now has the policemen with him wherever he goes. I do not see the good of this, for if the man intends to shoot him it makes little difference whether he is between two policemen or by himself.

The people who invited me to the last party are the Coppings; they are very nice people indeed. I met Miss C. and her cousin and several gentlemen from the party yesterday. I did not go in uniform - I wore a black stock. There were only two or three white neck-cloths there. Mrs. James is only about 20, I should think. She comes from Northamptonshire."

2nd Mar. 1847

"I spent this afternoon at the Assizes; there were fewer prisoners this year than there have been for a long time, which one would not have expected seeing the state the country is in. There is a great deal of fever and illness in the town and neighbourhood. The poor people are in a miserable state. Nearly every person you meet in the country begs of you. I am told there are a great number of people actually starving, but I do not think they are as bad in this County as at Skibereen and that neighbourhood. The ladies have had a bazaar here last Saturday for the poor people. I walked to Johnstown the other day, about 3 miles, to see the Castle, and the beautiful gardens and fountains, and the deer park. Altogether it is one of the nicest places I have ever seen. The owner, Mr. Grogan Morgan, is very rich, but a curious

fellow. He never sees anyone, not even his own family, and amuses himself every summer by pulling down part of his house and then building it up again. He seems to be pretty well liked."

10th Mar. 1847

"Today we went route-marching for the last time, for which I am rather sorry, but once the roads are dry they are so dusty that it makes very miserable work for the men. During the summer they will be drilled instead. The badge on our forage caps is to be done away with, and replaced by our Regimental number. We think the badge looks very much smarter, but we have no business wearing it; it was the Colonel's doing, but the authorities have only just noticed it. We still do not know if it will be 64 or LXIV. I was glad to hear that the length of service in India is to be reduced because they say we are going there about October next year.

If you go to the Louth Steeplechase I expect you will see all my Uncles. I hope you will be able to tell me that Uncle William has won on Oily Gammon. The days are much lighter now but it is not yet light enough to have dinner without candles."

20th Mar. 1847

"I was very disappointed to learn from your nice long letter that Oily Gammon did not run in the Louth Steeplechase. Perhaps Repealer will make up for it by winning at Lincoln."

27th March 1847

"It is fine weather for getting the crops in, but very few people are working the land. I do not know what they will do next year. The Wexford paper says that the Landlords in this county have all agreed not to give the small farmers any seed, but to make them give up their land and so get them off the land. Half the labourers on the Board of Works were discharged last week, so that they could work on the land instead, and it was expected there would be a row, but nothing has happened. I did not think I should have any pancakes for Shrove Tuesday, but Murphy brought me up six, which was very good of him. The priest gave it out at the Chapel what the people are allowed to eat during Lent. I suppose the poor people have never been allowed to eat so much meat before. They are in a wretched state. James has received an order to give away to them all the soldiers' old bedding.

We all went to Church last Wednesday, being Ash Wednesday, but all the shops were open, and the market was held as usual. There was nothing going on here on St. Patrick's Day, on account of the famine, I should imagine. I heard one of the men say it was the slowest St. Patrick's Day he had ever known.

I have not heard any particulars of the murders at Kilkenny; the men have not been found out yet. The poor man is supposed to have shot one of them, as one of his pistols had been discharged, and a man was found near the place wounded, but he says he was walking past and the other men shot him, and they cannot get anything else out of him. I should think this murder will frighten Mr. Hunt a little; he still drives about with his policemen."

2nd Apr.1847

"I marched the Roman Catholics to Chapel this morning at 10 o'clock. It was a very long service with a sermon, so we did not get back till 12.45 am so I could not get to Church. It was the first sermon I have heard. He talked such nonsense, saying things which are not in the Bible, and explaining others in a way I could not believe - but the people are not allowed to have bibles, are they not? They do not like the soldiers to hear any sermons, because they are usually on political subjects, so they send them at 10 o'clock when there is usually nothing but mass, so we get back at 11am and I then go with the other men to Church."

I was very sorry to hear from Uncle Fred that Repealer has not won Lincoln, as it was a capital stake. He came in third. He ran a very good race carried 7 pounds more than his weight. I hope he may win at Burton Constable next week. Owing to everything being so dear the poor soldiers are only having two meals a day, breakfast and dinner, and the first only a poor one.

When we are marching we do not have to pay anything for our beds. Five shillings a day is not much, but is better than nothing. I call upon Mrs. James now and then. The bushes are beginning to bud, but you scarcely ever see any thorn hedges here, they are all furze. I saw two swallows the other day; it is very soon for them, is it not? I do not know what can have made my last letter smell so nice. It must have been near one with violets in it in the letter bag. My money goes on much better here than it did at Kilkenny. I do not care how long we stay here.

We are having beautiful weather. The countryside is looking beautiful, the furze are in flower and smell very sweetly. There is nothing like as much fever in the town now. The crops are looking well, especially the beans. I often think of how I used to enjoy my walks with you especially at this time of year. Our Barrack Master died last week and was buried at a village about 5 miles from here. We were invited to the funeral. The men went without arms and James and I wore our red coats, and a great number of gentlemen followed him out of the town on foot as well as a long line of coaches. He had been ill for some time and had only been in the Barracks once or twice since we came here. He was 78.

The Colonel visited us a few days since, and so we got some news from Headquarters. The troops are not to be relieved until the autumn for fear that the soldiers should get the fever at the houses where they are billeted, and as the people are so poor it would be best both for them and the men, and very likely the detachments will not be relieved next month for the same reason. I should be happy to stay here three or four months longer.

You ask how much pay the soldiers get. Each man gets 1s. 1d. a day, and 8½d is deducted each day for his meals, pipe clay and washing. They cannot keep back more than that, and as everything is so dear now it is not enough to pay for their regular rations (1lb. of bread and ¾lb. of meat) so they have been having only two meals a day. Now the Government is going to pay the difference. They get their bread in the morning so they can divide it amongst the different meals as they like. They have a basin of coffee to breakfast and another at teatime. With the remainder of their money (4½d) they have to find everything that belongs to them except their uniform. So you can imagine that they do not have much pocket money. Mrs. Murphy always washes and mends my things very nicely, and I pay her at the end of the month.

What a great deal of change the railway will bring. I hear that Uncle William had his breakfast at Healing, went on the railway to Derby Agricultural Show and was back at Healing for breakfast by five o'clock next morning!"

11th April 1847

"I had one of my bad headaches on Friday, the first I have had since October. I had had a nasty pain across my right eye for two or three days, and did not feel very well. On Friday morning I could hardly see. I thought I knew what was the matter, and soon I had the most terrible headache. I managed to get Parade over, and then was very sick. I lay down on my bed, and thought what fun it was, but luckily I fell asleep at about ten o'clock, and did not wake till nearly four. My head was better, so I went for a short walk, and then went to James's for dinner. I took a good deal of medicine last night (probably senna, which seems to have been his preferred medication) *and I had three great thick dry toasts this morning to my breakfast, so you may fancy there is not much the matter with me now, dear Mama. I am not going to eat so much butter, as I blame it for the headache. At Kilkenny the other day the market was overstocked, and capital good potatoes were sold at 6d a stone. The farmers have held them till they found they would lose by it, and now are obliged to sell them cheap. Here they are between 14d and 16d a stone. They have been very good till last fortnight, and those I got last week were so bad that I have given them up.*

The wounded man that was found is dead, and just before his death he confessed that he was one of the murderers, and was the first who fired at the policeman. He would not say who the others were and they have not been found."

30th Apr. 1847

"We had a tremendous storm on Tuesday; the hailstones were the largest I have ever seen. There was one terrible thunderclap, which broke 10 windows in our Barracks, and struck a vessel in the harbour. The topmast was shivered to bits, and the lower part split right down to the deck. It is said that all the men on the Board of Works are to be discharged tomorrow."

10th May 1847

"I can just fancy Charley Banks riding one of their horses, wearing a shooting coat, a hat and a pair of spurs, with a great whip, and coming to School to ask Waite to give you a holiday. What a consequential fellow he must be now! The other day Nep (Neptune, Captain James's Newfoundland dog) *followed one of James's servants into the town, where a butcher's dog, which is a terrible fighter, was loose. They had a regular set-to. There were no soldiers about, so the butcher's boy helped his dog, but some people who saw it would not stand for it, and threatened to kick him if he did not let the dogs alone. They managed to separate them. A man had hold of Nep's tail and was pulling him back when the other silly fellow let the butcher's dog go. It went for Nep again, and seemed to give him a terrible bite on the cheek, except there is not a mark on him. The butcher says his dog is half worried.*

The General was at Kilkenny on Monday for the half-yearly inspection, and we are expecting him here any day now."

15th May 1847

There were still occasions when the troops had to assist the civil authorities. Enniscorthy, 14 miles from Wexford, had been a centre of the most violent resistance to the British in the 1798 rising of the United Irishmen, and had been held by the Irish for four weeks against attacks by General Draper's troops. Vinegar Hill, on the edge of the town, had been the site of the last bloody action of the rising, when the British artillery had massacred the Irish, led by Father John Murphy.

"About a week ago nearly 200 people went round to the country gentlemen and seized their sheep, and made them give them money. One gentleman had been giving them meal all winter and doing everything he possibly could for them. They went to him, and he gave them money, and a few

Old Kilkenny, an engraving c1850.

nights later they slaughtered and carried off ever so many of his sheep.

On Friday morning at 2.30 am Murphy woke me and said that a policeman had just come from Enniscorthy asking for help and that I was to take some men there. So I dressed as quickly as I could and had some breakfast. James came round to see that everything was in order, and I set off at four o'clock with a Sergeant and 20 men. I imagined from all accounts that we should have to use a few rounds of ball-cartridge, and was quite surprised to find the town perfectly quiet, but the magistrates had every reason to expect a row, and if they had not sent for us, and the people had assembled, they would have had time to pull the town down, before we could have got there. I enjoyed the march there very much; it is a capital road through pretty countryside

When we arrived I put the men into the Court House, and I took possession of the Magistrates' Room. Captain Kelly, the Government Inspector for the town, kindly gave me some breakfast. The Magistrates were examining some men about duck-stealing, but they had heard that posters had been put up all round the district, telling the people to assemble in the town, because all the men had been discharged from the public works, and the soup kitchens were not ready for them, and would not be for a week. They must be in a sad state, and they thought that by assembling in the town they could frighten the Magistrates into giving them provisions. About 100 of them went to one of the Magistrates who lives in the country, and on his promising to write to the Government for them, they went away quietly.

Nobody seemed to have come into the town so the Magistrates had a consultation and decided to keep us for another day. The men were billeted in houses, and I put up at the hotel, but dined with Capt. Kelly who kindly lent me some hairbrushes and things. In the morning the Magistrates promised the people to give them a supply of meal every day until the soup kitchens were ready, and we started for Wexford at about 2pm. It rained all the time we were marching, so we were pretty well soaked by the time we got in. As we came back into the town the old women in the market laughed at us, and kept asking, "Well, did you make pace? Where are all the boys? Did you get a good ducking?"

The Regiment has moved to Templemore, and we are to march there on Wednesday, halting at Callan on Sunday, and reaching Templemore on Tuesday. I shall be sorry to leave this place."

23rd May 1847

"We bid adieu to Wexford at 8.30 am Wednesday leaving four men to take care of the Barracks until a Company of the 83rd arrived. Mrs. James had been taken very ill on Monday and James could not leave her, so I was on my own. It was fine for our march, and we reached Taghmon at 11.30. It began to pour with rain in the afternoon so I was obliged to sit in the miserable little hotel, but they got me a paper and gave me a very comfortable dinner. The baggage went to Ross, and as Murphy

The Devil's Nick at Templemore, where the 64th Regiment did their musketry training. Local legend says that the Devil bit a chunk out of the ridge, and spat it out, when it became the hill of Cashel.

is a very bad marcher he was one of the baggage guard. On Thursday we started at 8 am and got to Ross at about two o'clock. A man with the bagpipes was going to Ross so he marched with us, all the men subscribing for him. He played nearly all the way and four or five of the men sang so we got on capitally.

There is a troop of the Bays at Ross, also a subaltern's detachment of the 15th. I had a good dinner of salmon and rhubarb tart. The next day we had a long hot march to Thomastown. Capt. Mildmay of the Bays was there, waiting for the Lord Lieutenant's funeral. I met him once when he dined in the Mess at Kilkenny. It would have been a dull evening without him. He had brought some wine with him, and we had a very good dinner. The funeral did not arrive until 2 am. There was a Hearse with 6 horses, four carriages with 4 each, and Capt. Mildmay's troop escorted it on to Bessborough.

Today we marched here, to Callan. It was the hottest day we have had this year. The men's faces are terribly burnt, my lips are quite skinned, and my face is as red as fire. James came over from Kilkenny to see how we were getting on. They call this a town but it is only a large village, with a very small hotel. I have a good room to myself and altogether am very comfortable. I have been accustomed to sit by myself lately. Uncle used to laugh at my hard feet, but I have found what a good thing it is. My feet never trouble me on the longest march. We shall be the last of the detachments to rejoin at Templemore. I am writing this with a steel pen, which I found here. It is perhaps a very good one but I cannot write well with them. There is a Lieutenant Crow of he Engineers here but I have not seen much of him."

28th May 1847

"On Monday morning James joined us and we started off on the 14 miles to Killinaule, the most miserable little place you ever saw. While we were there a man drove up in a dogcart, with three policemen with their bayonets fixed. He had a double-barreled shotgun, and when he came into the house he put a brace of pistols on the table beside him. I thought he must be a man who had been shot at and was being protected, but he was a Pay Clerk on the Board of Works. He is a regular fear-naught good-tempered fellow, and seems to care nothing for being shot at. After dinner a crowd of Engineers came in, and were drinking whiskey until 2 am, and making as much noise as only Irishmen can.

Next morning we did 10 miles to Thurles, rather a nice place. They had fever at the hotel so we were billeted at a grocer's. We had a splendid march of only 9 miles to reach here, at Templemore in beautiful weather, with everything so green. I have never seen anything like the orchards, all a mass of blossom. Altogether we marched 84 English miles from Wexford to Templemore.

These are splendid barracks, with two large squares, and all the buildings are three storeys high. The officers' quarters are very good, with all the rooms newly papered and painted. My rooms are on the top floor, with a beautiful view, though Murphy makes a fuss about having so many stairs to climb. The town is a wretched place, though it is silly to call it a town, when it is only the same size as Binbrook. (A village in the Lincolnshire Wolds, where the Lofts often stayed with the Iles family) *There is only one street with three or four respectable shops. Many of the fellows get*

The entrance to Templemore Barracks.

their things from Thurles. There are only 11 of us here - the Colonel, a Major, 2 Captains and 5 subs, but one of them is still on drill, so there are only 4 of us for duty. We have 300 men. The 70th share the Barracks with us. They have 500 men but 300 of them are recruits.

We are hoping to start a Cricket Club. There is a capital field close to the Barracks. There is to be a Steeplechase on Monday between an officer of the Engineers and one of the 70th. I am reckoning very much of it. As yesterday was the Queen's Birthday we had a grand Field Day and Feu de Joie. We marched out to a field with Colours flying and both bands playing - Godley and I carried our Colours. We fired three rounds and then took off our chacos and gave three cheers, taking out time from our Colonel. The Colonel and Adjutant of the 70th amused us very much as their horses were very bad to manage during the firing, and when the shouting began they both bolted.

Sir John Cardyne has a fine park close to the town, which he allows people to walk in. I believe it is very pretty but I have not been in it yet. One other person has a very nice house and grounds not far from the barracks, but these are the only nice houses anywhere near the town. The crops here are looking well, but I am afraid the potatoes are going again. There is a large field near the barracks where they are all diseased. We have two posts a day from Dublin, and two posts out."

30th May 1847

"I was as usual very much pleased to receive your nice long letter, which I did last night while at Mess, where I am Vice this week, and tomorrow I shall be President. I had plenty of carving at Wexford but the style there was not first rate. I like these barracks very much indeed. All the barracks are being papered, which make them look very comfortable, but I am afraid our barrack damages will be rather heavy. (Apparently the cost of papering the rooms would be deducted from the officers' pay.) *I have got two very good rooms on the third story over the Mess. Murphy makes a fuss about having to run up and down three flights of stairs so often, but it does not bother me. There are two windows looking onto the square, with a good view over the town and the Church, which has a spire something like Louth. The service starts at 10 o'clock, two hours earlier than the usual time. Today we did not go to Church as it was pouring with rain, so the Garrison Chaplain read prayers to our men and then gave us a short sermon in the Library. We send a night patrol of a sub and 16 men out twice a week; they have to stay out for four hours but need not march more than two miles in an hour. It will soon be my turn. Captain James has left Mrs. James in Kilkenny because there are no rooms for her here.*

A short time ago the railway bridge at Kilkenny collapsed. Lieutenant Crow whom I met at Callan had marched his Company under it just 5 minutes before. Was it not a lucky escape? Do you remember the clergyman who preached that Sunday you were at Kilkenny? He owed a great deal of money, and a short time since he bolted taking with him all the money that belonged to his sister which was in his hands, leaving the poor thing without a shilling. One of the Dean of Kilkenny's sons, who used often to dine with us, was caught cheating at cards at a Club in Dublin by the Colonel of the Scotch Greys, who then kicked him down stairs. The poor Dean was in a sad state. I believe the son is going to go to Australia; they say he has been at it for a long time.

When our HQ left Kilkenny they were burying 25 people a day out of the Fever Hospital. Our Mess cook died of it, but fortunately very few of the soldiers took it. 60 of our men and two officers from Thurles were out on Friday collecting the rents from the farmers and evicting those who would not pay. We are going to send out a party on the same duty tomorrow."

4th June 1847

"It has been very hot recently and we have had a great deal of drill. Two of the men fainted on parade yesterday. The 70th dined with us on Wednesday. 25 of us sat down at 7.30, which is their dinner hour and managed without candles. The Barrack Master's daughter has been very ill, so we have not been able to have the Band or the fifes and drums in the evening, for fear of disturbing her, but the poor girl died on Tuesday so we had the Band playing in the Ante-room, and had a capital dinner.

The crops around here are looking most beautifully, but I am afraid the potatoes are going again. There is a large field not far from this where they are all diseased. I have been sitting on a Court Martial for the last three days."

Templemore Barracks.

23rd June 1847

"Our Colonel has gone on leave, a thing he seldom does, and we expect he will be back before his leave has expired. I do not know what our Colonel will do if we go to India. He has served long enough to retire on full pay if he likes, but he is not at all anxious to leave the service; besides, he is rather a great man now, and if he retires he will be nobody. We have plenty of music now. The 70th band plays on Mondays and Thursdays, and ours during dinner on Wednesdays and on Friday evening. I think their band is the best band to march to, and ours for the softer sort of music in the evenings. The 70th have black velvet facings, and small black stripes on the gold lace of their skirt ornaments, and their Band and Drum Majors are dressed exactly like ours. They are terrible-looking fellows with their great bearskin caps.

I wrote to Macdonoe the other day to order an Invisible Green coat with silk linings, as I fancied I should like that colour best. Do you remember me telling you of those two men who deserted in March? When they were taken they had their firelocks loaded. They were sentenced to two years imprisonment with hard labour. Everyone is surprised they were not transported."

There seems to have been a certain ambivalence in Harry's views on the way the authorities dealt with the problem of non-payment of rent by Irish tenants. He seemed to be more sympathetic to the tenants while he was at Wexford than he was once he was back with a greater number of fellow-officers at Templemore.

"We have a Captain and two Lieutenants very ill on sick leave. We are not going to send out any more patrols; the countryside is so quiet that they are no longer needed. They were to arrest any illegal armed parties and to go to the assistance if any houses were attacked, but they have never had anything to do. There has been no further word about ejectment parties. You need have no fear about our being in danger. The people dare not do anything against us. The 92nd are now at Enniskillen, and are expecting to march to Dublin before long. Singleton and Du Cane are both on detachment, so I usually go out with Burne or Godley, who are both very nice fellows. Mrs. James is now in barracks, but I don't think they can be very comfortable, as they have only got one quarters, the same size as mine."

7th June 1847

Sometimes Harry addressed his letters to his brother, James, whom he usually called Jem, especially if he had news which he thought would interest James rather than his mother. She told Harry: *"Jem will not let me open a letter from you, so I have to wait until he comes home from school for breakfast to find out your news."* This is one of the letters addressed to Jem:

"Now that our Colonel is on leave Colonel Bigge of the 70th commands the garrison. He has had us defending the walls, with the men pretending to fire through the loop-holes, forming again in the square, then rushing off once more to the walls,

which they defended in such gallant style that the enemy was soon driven off.

On Monday Godley and I went to see the Steeplechase. There were between 300 and 400 people there. It was a very hot day and with the hedges and trees so green, and a lot of flowers it did not look much like steeplechasing weather."

Several pages follow giving a detailed description of the course, and a very full account of the race itself, which was won by Wilson of the 70th, to the disappointment of the crowd, who supported the Engineer, because he rode in green colours.

"There are 4 or 5 quite high mountains about 5 miles from here, and in one of them there is a large gap, which they say was caused by the Devil biting a chunk out of it, so it called the Devil's Bit. Last Monday Burne and I climbed to the top of it, from which we had a most beautiful view, which included the Shannon on the other side. We could also see Nenagh, which I recollect Mama used to know. (It was at Nenagh that Margaret and her husband had gathered the bunch of wild flowers on the day before they left Ireland). *The country on this side is very nicely wooded, but perfectly flat, and on the other side it is all hills. As we were about half way up we asked a young fellow, how far it was to the top. "Oh", he said, "not far, your honour. You will not feel yourself go up this bit". It was very hot and very steep, so we felt it quite a lot! On the way down we stopped at the young fellow's house, and he milked the cow for us, and we drank such a lot of new milk. It was the first I had tasted for a long time. Do you remember walking to Grainsby for the first time at this season of the year? I reckon very much on walking that road again with you.*

Did I tell you about the bailiff being murdered at Thurles about a fortnight since? The Sheriff had turned some people out of their houses and put locks on the doors, but they went into them again. For doing so they are liable to arrest. This poor

The bailiffs' visit in Ireland, from a contemporary Victorian print.

fellow went to summons them for the Assizes, but the wretches murdered him and buried his body. 60 of our men and 50 policemen went out the next day and arrested 11 men who were suspected. One of them was all covered in blood, and they found the scythe with which he was murdered, which was also stained with blood. The houses were then knocked down, and the men taken to prison. The body was found soon after; they had cut his head off. We had a Field Day on Monday and fired 15 rounds of blank cartridge."

19th June 1847

"We sent out another ejectment party of 50 men and 2 officers on Wednesday. They were out all day and it was pouring with rain. Nearly all the people paid and very few houses were knocked down. It seems a cruel way of behaving, but it is the only way. One man they turned out had had a house and land for 25 years, and had only paid £3 rent the whole time."

2nd July 1847

"After all the delays General Sir Charles Napier finally arrived here and yesterday inspected the Regiment. Murphy got some curious idea into his head, and called me at 5 am, which was hardly necessary, as I did not have to be on parade until 8 am. We were in our blue coats, and Godley and I carried the Colours, as we were the only Ensigns. At 8.30 we were drawn up in line, and the General came on the ground. We saluted him, and he then inspected the men. It was a fearfully hot day, and one of the men fainted while standing in the ranks. We marched past in slow and quick time, and then the Colonel put us through a few movements. The General was pleased with us, and said he would not have been so particular with us, if he had not heard a great deal about us in Dublin, and wanted to see if it could be true. After the inspection he, his secretary, his aide de camp and the Colonel of the 70th breakfasted with us. He is a very fine looking old man, very good-tempered, with long white hair, and a very large swelling under his right ear. He lost his left arm in the Peninsula, and now commands the Limerick District. His aide de camp is one of our Lieutenants, 6' 4" tall, who looks remarkably well in his Staff uniform. It was he who had told the General what a good Regiment ours is. After breakfast he inspected the barracks and the men's dinners, and then went on to inspect the 70th, who were in full dress. Seven of their men fainted. He had luncheon in their Mess.

This lovely hot weather will bring on the crops nicely. They were all busy leading the hay yesterday. Pilleau, the Surgeon of the 70th, asked me if Mrs. Thomas Kilner (Margaret's sister) *was my aunt. Have you ever heard of him? I have been reading a very good book, called "The Romance of War" or "The Highlanders in Spain". It is an account of the 92nd during the Peninsular War. Have you read it? There are three volumes now, but I saw in the paper an advertisement of the fourth. As you may fancy I was much interested in it."*

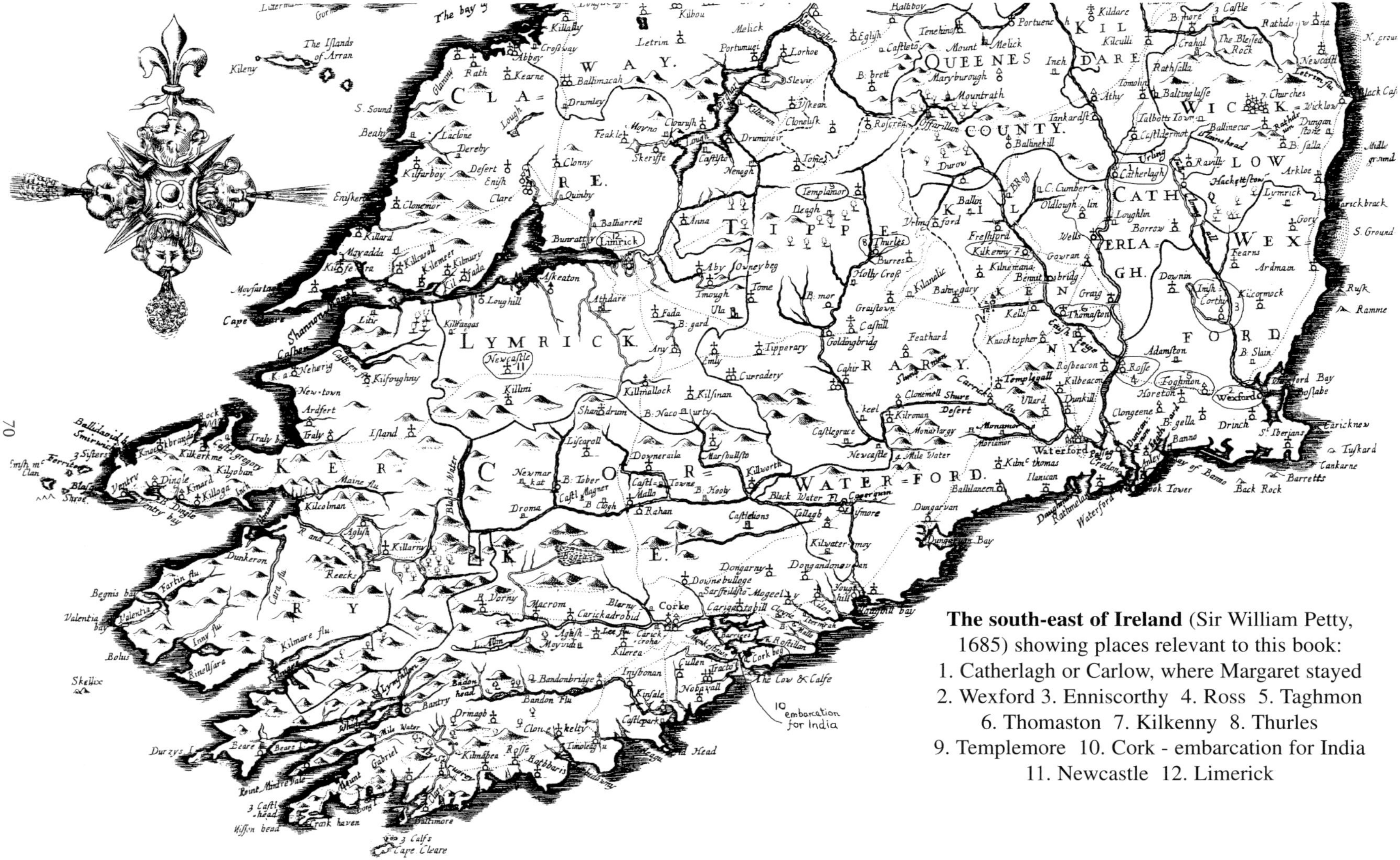

The south-east of Ireland (Sir William Petty, 1685) showing places relevant to this book:
1. Catherlagh or Carlow, where Margaret stayed
2. Wexford 3. Enniscorthy 4. Ross 5. Taghmon
6. Thomaston 7. Kilkenny 8. Thurles
9. Templemore 10. Cork - embarcation for India
11. Newcastle 12. Limerick

7th July 1847
There are comparatively few references to real military training in the Regiment.

"This morning we have been out ball-firing nearly to the top of the Devil's Bit: it is the only place near here where we can fire without running the risk of shooting somebody. We started at 9 am and got back by 1 pm; it was raining nearly all the way there, and we had some heavy showers as we came back, so we all got pretty well drenched. We shall have one of these excursions every week now, I expect.

Mr. Cardyne, who has been shot at so often, dined with the 70th last week. He walked home at about 11 pm, with a double-barrelled gun slung across his back, and a brace of pistols in his pocket. His house is about two miles from here, but he thought he should be more likely to get there on foot than in his carriage. He is trying to get all the people out of their farms, and make them into labourers, which is why they are so anxious to shoot him. They say that having so many enemies is the reason for him not being shot, for everyone leaves it for the others to do, and so he escapes altogether; whereas if he had only a few, he would be shot at once.

I should think you would see that the wounded man who was found, is dead. Just before he died he confessed that he was one of the murderers, and was the first who fired at the policeman, and poor Brown shot him. He would not say who the others were, and nothing has been heard of them.

I got my paletot last Saturday; I like the colour very much indeed, and I am glad I got the silk lining. I should have liked the coat better if it had not been quite so wide, and if the pockets had been at the sides, but it is a very nice coat. Altogether I like it here. My room is nearly at the end of the house, and is not far from the Band room, so I can hear them very plainly indeed when they are practising.

Last Friday I walked to Thurles, to get some money, as there is no bank here. I started at 2 pm and got there at 4 pm only to discover that the bank was closed, and I had to walk another 9 miles back, on a very dirty road, under a blazing hot sun. I was nearly wet through when I got back. Yesterday I had the pleasure of sitting on a Court Martial to try a poor private of the 70th. There were 14 members, and the President, Brevet Colonel Maclean of the 72nd Highlanders, who is a very curious fellow. When the General went to Nenagh to inspect his Regiment, he wanted the two Ensigns to stand with the Colours on two pillars on either side of the barracks gate, but they would not do so. So he sent up two pipers, who tried all they could to blow the General out of the square.

I am glad that Uncle William Martin has arrived. Tell Mama that if he wants to see me, the railway is now open to Maryborough, there is a coach to Roscrae, and you have to get a car from there to Templemore."

Harry had been looking forward to meeting his uncle who was in England for the first time. Unfortunately things did not turn out as he hoped.

Ireland in the 1840s.
The Great Famine, from 1845, caused terrible suffering for the Irish Catholic population. British soldiers were stationed there in great numbers to maintain the peace, although while Harry was there things were quieter than at any time in the previous 20 years - the Irish had probably been starved into submission at the time.

Soup schools provided soup and protestantism to catholics.

Irish rebels.
A small uprising in 1848 was soon quelled.

Emigrant ships.
The solution for many Irish catholics was emigration to America

CHAPTER 5

FAMINE FEVER

As Harry's letter indicated, Margaret's brother, William Martin, was in England on a long furlough from Tobago where he was the Manager and Attorney of two sugar plantations. It was the first time that he had met his family since he had sailed for Tobago in 1833, at the age of 16. William, known as Uncle Willie to distinguish him from Uncle William Loft, was planning to come to Dublin with his nephew James, and hoped that Harry might get a few days leave, so that he could join them there. However Willie's plans kept being changed because of his business commitments in London, Glasgow, and Aberdeen.

Unfortunately on 16th July, Harry was struck down by 'Famine Fever' and all their plans had to be changed. Some privates of the 64th, and also some of the 70th, who were in the same barracks, had contracted the disease, and shortly afterwards Harry's Company Commander, Captain James, was also struck down, not as severely as Harry.

23rd July 1847
The Regimental Surgeon, Dr Smith, wrote to Margaret saying:

"This day week your son was seized by the prevailing fever, which is still present, though considerably abated. He has had a great deal of headache, and also some cough, but he has not been delirious. He is a good deal pulled down, but he will soon get over that when a more generous diet can be allowed him."

26th July 1847
Three days later he wrote again to say:

"Your son is rather better, with less fever. His headache has gone, but there is still some cough, with uneasiness in his chest, to relieve which a blister was applied last night. He is in good spirits, taking arrowroot and sago. As the quickness of pulse and heat of the skin abate I shall give him beef tea and wine in the way of support. The fever prevalent in this country at present follows a determinate course, lasting generally from 9 to 21 days. Your son has now been ill for ten days. His servant is very careful and attentive as a nurse, and rest assured that every attention in my power shall be paid to him."

Margaret was obviously extremely worried. She wrote to Harry:

"I shall write to you every other day till you are able to get about again, as I think it will amuse you. I fear you will be very dull and lonely being so many hours by yourself. How much I wish I could transport myself to you. I feel so restless and unsettled that I cannot be there to nurse you. I shall not cross my letters for the time being, in case they should cause your head to ache. Will you offer my best thanks to

Dr. Smith for his kindness in writing, which has been a great comfort and relief to me? Be sure to get everything that is right and proper, never mind the expense. Be very particular in doing nothing but what the Doctor allows and approves of. I am so sorry to think of you not being able to get a lemon in Templemore, as I fear you will have equal difficulty in getting other things which would tempt your appetite."

In spite of her stated intention Margaret not only 'crossed' this letter, but also wrote inside the flap of the envelope!

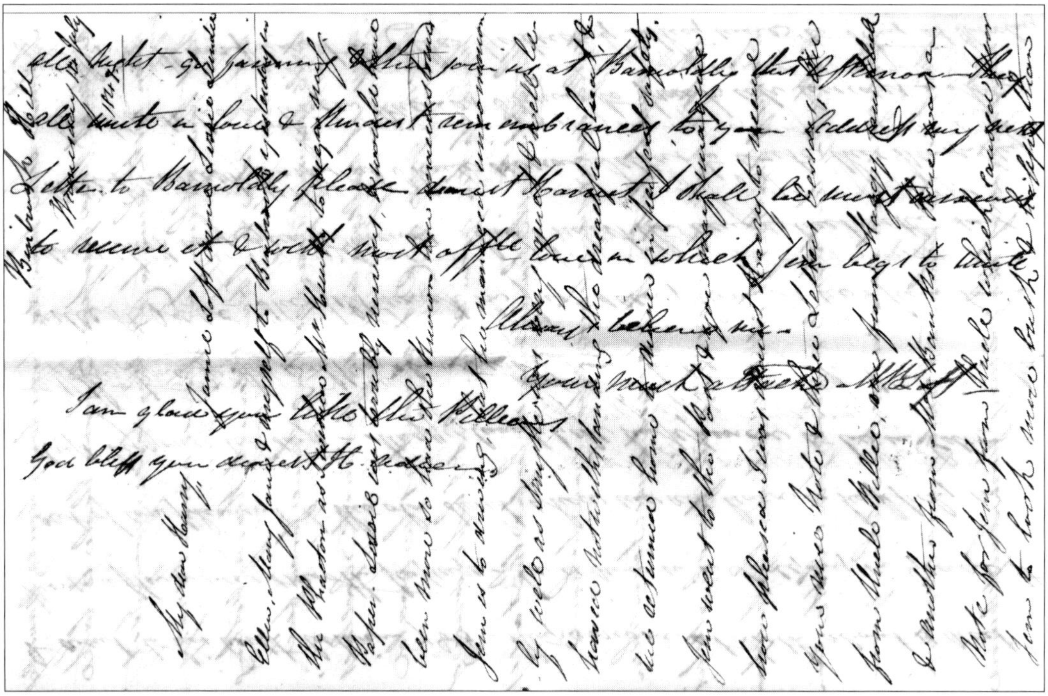

A letter from Margaret Loft to Harry, in her beautiful copperplate writing, showing how she 'crossed' the pages in order to get as much as possible on each page, to reduce the cost of postage. She always signed her letters "Your much attached Mother, Margaret B. Loft.

2nd August 1847

This was the first letter Harry wrote after his illness.

"The fever has left me for nearly a week, and they are now giving me weak brandy and water, (I like it better than wine) broth and jelly, so I hope I shall soon be strong again. I had a chop this morning. Dr. Smith has gone on leave for 2 months, and I am now under the care of the Asst. Surgeon, Dr. Purdeau. He is a M.D. and a very clever young man. I am afraid this illness had removed any chance of my visit to Dublin. I should have enjoyed it very much."

12th August 1847

"I am still weak but stronger than I was, but I sit up now for 4 hours at different times during the day. I do not intend to buy a wig to be used merely for a couple of

weeks. It is nearly three weeks since my head was shaved, and my hair is only just long enough for anyone to get hold of it. I am able to read now which is a great comfort."

Margaret agreed with Harry.

"You are quite right in not getting a wig; your hair will soon grow and all the more rapidly for being exposed to the air. You should put plenty of castor oil on it."

21st August 1847

"I am much stronger now, and yesterday I walked down the stairs to the Ante-Room by myself. My legs trembled and felt wobbly, but I managed it very well. My appetite is very good. I have 5 meals a day, and could easily eat two or three more. I sleep much better now that I get up during the day. Captain James has had the fever five or six days after I did, but it was not such a severe attack. He has been out driving for more than a week. We have had 6 or 7 men in the nearby hospital ever since we came here.

Harry added some advice on his brother's clothes.

"I think Jem is quite big enough for a coat, but he would then want stick-ups, a hat instead of a cap, and different other things, so a jacket would be cheaper."

Wearing a tailcoat instead of a short jacket, starched collars instead of soft turned-down ones, and a hat instead of a cap, were the signs of approaching manhood for well-brought up young males.

27th August 1847

"I got out onto the square last Sunday for the first time for a short time. I walked up and down and then had a ride on Purdeau's mare. I intend now to go out every day. We are having beautiful weather for the harvest"

Meanwhile his brother James sailed from Hull to Leith, and then travelled to Glasgow where he met his uncle William Martin. They were on the point of crossing to Dublin when they learned that Harry had already left Ireland for Lincolnshire on sick leave, having got over the worst of the fever. His weight had fallen to 9 stone 8 pounds, but he felt he was regaining some of his strength, and was fit to travel.

Uncle William was rather cross that he had not been told earlier of this new development. He took James for a short tour of Loch Lomond and the Trossachs before returning to Louth on the 9th where the whole family was reunited.

Harry spent the next few weeks convalescing. Margaret was overjoyed to have her brother and both her sons all under one roof. There was so much news to catch up on, that everyone seemed to be talking all the time. William was surprised to find that Margaret was no longer 'Meg' to anyone except himself, just as their sister, Christina, was no longer 'Kit', and they had both lost much of their Scottish speech. The Europeans in Tobago were mostly Scottish so William had retained his accent. Margaret found it hard to accept that William was no longer the boy he was when they last met, but a 30 year old man, whose business experience and acumen was appreciated by her male friends, while her female friends were struck by his handsome appearance and elegant clothes

Margaret was sad when William left, but was pleased to see how well Harry was recovering under the care of Dr. Banks, and was delighted to be able to take him round to see all their old friends. Best of all as far as Harry was concerned, was staying with the uncles, John and William Loft, at Healing.

During this time Margaret received news from Mrs. Norris, a Louth friend who was the sister-in-law of Captain Norris of the 64th, that there was going to be a vacancy for a Lieutenant in the Regiment, as Lieutenant Carter was to get his Company. She at once started to write to everyone who might be able to assist in obtaining the promotion for Harry, who knew nothing of her plans, and might well have been horrified if he had known. She wrote not only to Captain James but also to Colonel Stretton himself to enquire if there was a chance of Harry getting his 'step-up', and also of succeeding Carter as Adjutant. They both replied politely, though very formally in the Colonel's case, to say that no vacancy without purchase would occur, and that Thompson was going to purchase the promotion, while Burne was to be the new Adjutant.

25th October 1847
Harry had obtained a certificate from Dr Banks, supporting an extension of his sick leave. He was staying at Healing, from which place he wrote to his mother:

"I had rather a cold drive to New Holland (the landing stage for the Humber ferry) *yesterday as the wind meeting us all the way. We got to Hull at about 11.30 am. Uncle John was there to meet me and we went at once to the Garrison. Mr. Jackson was very friendly and asked me a few questions and then copied out Dr. Banks's certificate. I wrote out my formal application and posted it. Then I had some dinner with George and Henry* (sons of his father's cousin, Richard Lundie, who was the Governor of Hull Gaol), *left for New Holland about 3.30 pm and reached Riby crossroads where Crisp was waiting for me with a horse. I was rather tired by it all."*

It seems to have been a very energetic day for a man who was applying for more sick leave. Harry was granted the extension of his sick leave, but at the end of November he had to return to duty. It was a bitterly cold morning with snow on the ground. Margaret was much distressed by his departure and wrote:

"I stood at the door listening to your receding footsteps until you got out of Brett's passage. Everything was so still and quiet I could hear them distinctly. I heard you blow your nose when you got nearly to the bottom of the street. I stood at the door until the clock struck the quarter to five as I hoped to hear the wheels of the coach as it drove along Mercer Row. In this however I was disappointed, and with a sad heart I went into the house again and returned to bed, but did not get to sleep

again for a long time. It was a long, dull, dreary, day. I was very glad when it was 4 o'clock that I might go to Walker (the driver of the Grimsby coach) *to enquire whether you reached Grimsby in time for the train."*

1st December 1847

"This is a short note to say that I did not arrive here until 6 o'clock this morning, but the Colonel did not say anything about it, so it does not matter. I expect to go on detachment to Croombe in a few days. On Monday they told me the hare had been put on the coach, but when we had gone some way Walker said he had never seen it. He promised to take it the next day and deliver it to Uncle Lundie, free of any charge. My bed is being aired before a good fire."

3rd December 1847

Harry's journey had been a long one, lasting just over two days and involving two coaches, three ships, and two trains. Grimsby was still a small tidal port, so the coach from Louth was timed to coincide with the high tide, which was the only time that vessels could enter and leave the port.

"I have now time to give you a full account of my journey. At Holton it began to pour with freezing rain. I was on the box but did not get at all wet. I caught the packet with a little time to spare, but we were delayed by two vessels in the out-fall at Grimsby and did not get out into the river till 8 o'clock. We reached Hull at a quarter to nine. The Lundies were very kind and gave me some breakfast. Uncle saw me to the train, and offered me some potted meat to eat on the journey, but my pockets were full, and I could not very well have scooped it up with my fingers, so only had some of the plum bread before I reached Liverpool at quarter to six.

I had a very good and cheap dinner at an eating house, and took a cab to the docks. A small steamer took us out to the "Princess" which was laying some distance out in the channel. I got to my cabin at 8 o'clock and was asleep almost at once. It was very rough and early in the morning I was rather sick but nothing to signify. Because of the head wind we were late reaching Kingstown at 10.15 am and the morning train for Ballybrophy had already departed, and the mail train did not leave till the evening. I had a meal and sat in the eating-house, reading the papers for a long time and had a walk before catching the train. I had another long wait at Ballybrophy in a little wooden house where they sell the tickets. There was a stove in it, which almost suffocated me, so the door had to be left open even though it was so cold. When the mail coach came at last they gave me some strange food and plenty of straw to keep my feet warm as I was travelling inside. We reached Limerick soon after six o'clock. I had some breakfast, had my boots cleaned, spruced myself up a little and then drove to the barracks. Carter took me to see the Colonel and I explained why I had returned late and he said it was of no matter."

Limerick was the largest place in which Harry had been stationed; an important industrial town at the head of the estuary of the Shannon, and the centre of a fertile farming area. During 1690 the Castle, under the dynamic leadership of the Irish patriot Patrick Sarsfield, had successfully withstood a siege by the forces of King William III, led by the Dutch General Ginkel. The next year the Castle had been forced to capitulate, when the opposing commanders drew up the Treaty of Limerick. It gave a limited amount of religious freedom to the Catholic population, and offered a safe passage abroad to the Irish soldiers. Although it received King William's approval, it was not ratified by the Irish Parliament. The Treaty Stone came to be regarded as a symbol of deceit and betrayal.

"The Castle Barracks are in the ruins of the Castle which withstood the famous siege. I am in the Strand Barracks, which are miserable ones. My room is a large cold one which they have been using as a schoolroom, as I expect to be on detachment in a few days. I have had little boys knocking at my door in the morning, imagining that it was still their schoolroom. The 92nd (Harry's father's old regiment) *are here, so I have a chance of seeing them. Limerick is a very fine town but a very dirty one. The people are said to be very stupid by people from other places. The river runs between the Castle and our Barracks. There are ten bridges over it and in one of them is a large stone, which they call The Treaty Stone, because the Treaty was signed on it. Murphy is at Croombe so I have Jeffery, a fatigue man, to see to my things.*

There was a man shot near here on Monday, and two policemen were fired at, but neither of them was much hurt. You may have seen in the paper an account of a clergyman being shot on his way home from Church last Tuesday."

11th December 1847

"James has got leave until the beginning of next month so some of our friends need not have made such a fuss about my getting three months. Armstrong got the fever after I left. He was very ill indeed, and the doctors gave him up for a time. He is better now and has gone on leave. Captain Lyttleton has got his step (promotion) *but the senior Lieutenant would not give enough money for it, so Lyttleton will not go yet."*

This is an illustration of the complexity of the system of promotion by purchase, which was to continue in the Army for another generation.

Harry's weight was again almost 12 stone, and he looked so fit, with a full round face, that he had to put up with a lot of chaff from his comrades about malingering. As he expected, he did not stay long in Limerick.

CHAPTER 6
REGIMENTAL LIFE

In addition to the rather meagre details of regimental duty contained in Harry's letters, some extra information can be gleaned from the Roll Book of his unit. The 64th Regiment had developed a Squad system. The Regiment was commanded by a Lieutenant Colonel, and divided into two Wings, each commanded by a Major. These were subdivided in turn into Companies, under the command of a Captain, further divided into two sub-divisions, each a Subaltern's command, and finally into Squads commanded by Sergeants, with a Corporal assisting each Sergeant, and, at least in theory, a Drummer for each Squad. So Harry was now responsible for the left Sub-division of Captain James's Company, consisting of Squads 3 and 4.

Harry liked his Captain, who was a highly respected and popular officer; his young wife, Susan, figured prominently in the social life of the Regiment. It was later to be a disappointment to Harry that Captain James was transferred to the elite Grenadier Company, and was replaced by Captain Pattison, who had been in the detachment on the Alert when it was wrecked on Goose Island.

Harry, still only 17, was in command of 42 men, 28 of them Irish, 8 Scottish, and 6 English. They were all older than he was, the average age being 26, but it may have been some compensation that at 6 feet he was almost 6" taller than most of them, and 2" taller than the tallest of them. Most of them had enlisted at about 18 years old, when they were described as labourers, with a few weavers, bricklayers, dyers, and one clerk. Of the Irish 20 were Catholic and 8 Protestant, while all the Scots and English were Protestant. Sixteen of them had been court-martialled at some time. Seven of them were married 'with leave' and six 'without leave'. Only men who had married with leave were entitled to have their wives with them. Harry's Sergeants were James Howell, a married man from Swaffham in Norfolk, aged 32, (almost twice as old as Harry) and Patrick O'Reilly, a single man from Enniskelling, aged 29, with 14 and 12 years service respectively. Their Corporals were John Hagherty, aged 27, from Derry, and James Wilson, aged 26, from Glasgow.

The fact that there were so many Irishmen, both Catholic and Protestant, in the regiment apparently presented no difficulty in using them to deal with disorder among the civilian population of Ireland. There seems to be some evidence that the Irish people regarded the Highland regiments with more hostility than the English ones. This was mentioned both by Harry and by his father. In political cartoons of the period, showing the state of the Irish peasantry, any soldier involved is frequently depicted in bonnet and kilt.

The Squad Book laid down that *"when the Company is formed and properly told off (previous to marching into column) the senior officer will take advantage of the spare time, by setting up the men, correcting their position if required, and practising them in the several Company formations; all of which tends to diminish the necessity of regular drills".* It was also insistent that *"every Subaltern must be well acquainted with the character, services, etc. of every man in his Sub-division, attend especially to their wants, visit them in hospital, and visit the Squad room at uncertain intervals."*

The maintenance of good feeling between officers and men was stressed, in order to prevent crime and consequently the need for punishment. From the evidence of the letters, this seems to have been an unrealised ideal, since Harry never mentions any dealings with privates or non-commissioned officers, except his servant, Murphy. The gulf between the officers and the other ranks was as great as in most units of the Army.

After rejoining the Regiment at Limerick Harry was quickly on detachment again.

13th December 1847

"On Saturday three Companies of the 92nd under Major Atherly marched into Limerick, and I and another fellow had to move from the Strand Barracks to the New Barracks to make room for them. It was a miserable wet day, and since HQ is in the Castle the two of us had to walk a mile and a half to dinner in the Mess. On Monday I was busy packing for the move. It was the most stormy day I ever saw. Windows, chimney pots and lamps were flying in all directions. Two men broke their arms by being blown into lampposts, and a woman was blown into a quarry.

I left Limerick in a public car and arrived here, at Croome, after a two-hour ride in a most fearful storm. I had my cap on and my greatcoat and my cloak, and sat with my back to the wind, but I was very cold and wet. When the rain stopped the wind dried everything so quickly that all my clothes were covered in dust. I never had such a journey in all my life. Murphy came the next day with the baggage. The other Companies of the 92nd under Major Thorold (Harry's godfather) *marched into Limerick the day after I left. Burne has taken command of the detachment."*

Captain James, the Company Commander, was still on sick leave. He complained that he had served in the notoriously unhealthy West Indies without a day's illness, and had then nearly died in Ireland. In his absence there were only two subalterns with the detachment. Margaret was alarmed that the detachment was such a small one, as the passing of the Arms Bill was thought likely to cause unrest. She was delighted to know that the 92nd Highlanders, her husband's old regiment, with her friends Major Thorold and Captain Sutherland still serving, was to be stationed with the 64th, but *"this wretched weather will be miserable for their poor cold knees".*

20th December 1847.

"Croome is a small, dirty, village about 12 miles from Limerick. There are no regular barracks or officers' quarters, so the men are quartered in two houses, and

Burne and I are allowed lodging money, (12/- a week each). We are living in a pretty good house, where we have two bedrooms and a furnished sitting room, for which we pay 22/- a week. They find us coals, and we have one of the soldiers' wives to cook for us. There is plenty of duty here, three patrols and two escorts a week. No officer is required for the patrols, but I come in for the escort duty every Tuesday and Friday. We have to escort flour from the mills here to a place three miles off, with 20 men and 12 carts. We start at about 10 am. and get back at about 2 pm.

An order came out lately that all escorts passing through towns where troops are stationed are to be inspected by an officer who has to give them a certificate stating he has done so, and if any escort does not get this certificate it is to be reported to the Adjutant General. Escorts are passing through this place all the time, so that one of us is obliged to be available always, which is a great bother. Sir Michael Cray, who commands all the troops round Cork, came over here yesterday to Church, and afterwards asked Burne to show him what accommodation there was here, in case any of his detachments have to fall back upon us! He spoke of our commanding position, and seemed to be expecting a row when the Arms Bill comes into operation, and said we should have a great deal of work here. A Captain of the 92nd sent Burne a note saying that he would probably relieve us next week. I hope he doesn't, as I have had plenty of moves lately, and am very comfortable here.

There are some very nice families in the neighbourhood who have been very civil to Burne, but none of them have called upon me yet, but I suppose they will, if we remain. There is a clergyman living here, Vicar of a parish a few miles off, who keeps a pack of hounds and hunts three times a week. That Captain Bartlett who had his helmet smashed with stones a short time since, was over here the other day and said he was going to keep some hunters in the stables belonging to this house."

Harry's next move entailed what would later be described as "a combined operation', with which they were all unfamiliar, and which was inevitably chaotic.

31st December 1847

"Here I am at Glin, a village on the Shannon, about 36 miles from Limerick. We got the route at Croome last Monday. I was not sorry to get out of the place. We were relieved by Captain Hames's Company of the 92nd. Captain Mackenzies' Company of the 92nd marched through on their way to Birr as we left. The Highlanders created a great sensation, as you may suppose. The people all came out of their houses and shouted. We got to Limerick at about 3.0 p.m. after a very wet march. There was no room for the men in barracks, so we were all billeted in the town. The next day we were busy having the men inspected, and seeing the baggage put on board the steamer. On Thursday morning we were called at 4.30 am, and were embarked by 6. It was a fine morning but very dark. The men had a large cabin, and Burne and I had a small one to ourselves, where we had some breakfast

The organisation and standing orders of the 64th Regiment.

The Squad System, as carried on in the 64th, Regiment.

1.—The *Lieutenant Colonel*, of course, is responsible for the discipline &c. of the whole Battalion.

2.—The *Majors*, each superintend a wing of the Battalion.

3.—The *Captain* superintends his Company.

4.—Each *Subaltern* superintends a subdivision or two squads.

5.—Each *Serjeant* superintends a squad, assisted by an equal proportion of Corporals.

The *Major* is responsible to the Commanding Officers for the preservation of the squad system, and the maintenance of due responsibility in his wing.

He is answerable also for the general discipline of the wing—for the cleanliness of the Barracks, and the regularity of the Company accounts.

The *Captain* is responsible to the Major of the wing for the same duties; but confined to his own Company, to the superintendence of his own Subalterns and Non-commissioned Officers, and also to the preservation of their respective responsibility.

The *Subalterns* must remain as much as possible with their own Companies and Squads, and *never* be changed, except on promotion or in consequence of some other permanent arrangement.

The *Non-commissioned Officers* and *men* should in like manner, be stationary with their squads, and should also be accommodated as near to each other as possible in Barracks, or Billets.

The *Major* will visit his half of the barracks, the Captain his company's rooms, and the Subaltern his squad rooms, at uncertain periods. The Subaltern must be acquainted with the character, services, &c. of every man in his subdivision—he must attend especially to their wants—and visit them occasionally in Hospital; in fact he should take a special interest in every thing connected with the men entrusted to his charge, as much as the Captain of the company.

By constantly retaining officers with their own men, an interest is created, and a good feeling maintained, such as should always exist between the officer and soldier—characters and dispositions are known and understood, all which tends greatly to diminish crime, and consequently the necessity of punishment.

If a Captain is absent for a short period, his Lieutenant must take charge of the company, and the Colour Serjeant of the subdivision, the Corporal of the squad, and thus the chain of responsibility will be preserved and maintained.

After the squads have been minutely inspected on Parade by the Subalterns, attended by the Non-commissioned Officers, the company must be formed and handed over to the Captain by the senior subaltern.

The *Captain* will be received with carried Arms, and the State at the same time be handed to him.

When the Company is formed and properly told off the senior Officer (previous to marching into column), will take advan tage of the spare time, by setting up his men, correcting their position if required, and practising them in the several company formations; all of which tends to diminish the necessity of regular drills.

The *Captain* should be always in possession of his company book, filled up upon this principle.

The *Subalterns* must each have books, containing their respective subdivisions, carefully made out, and the Non-commissioned Officers must severally be provided also with books of their respective squads, made out by themselves.

A company paraded in squad order, should stand according to the accompanying sketch.—Each Squad in rank entire—and at quarter distance.

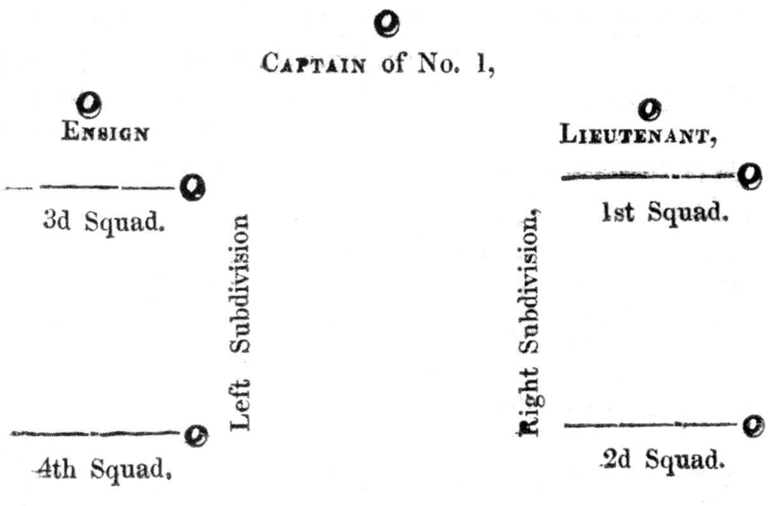

and the toughest steak I ever met with. It is a war steamer, which has been employed during the last year carrying supplies up and down the Shannon.

We arrived opposite Glin at about 10 am, but found there was no boat large enough to land us, so we went two miles further down the river to Tarbet to get a large boat from a man o'war anchored there. The wind and tide were both against us, so that we got on very slowly, and we were carried away from the vessel several times. It was nearly 3 pm when we got back to Glin, and raining hard. We got all the men in the large boat, and Burne. and I were in the ship's cutter, with four men and a Midshipman, and had the other boat in tow. It was very rough, and the large boat rolled very much, and the tide was very low. They tried to get up a gully, but there was not enough water, so the men had to jump overboard and wade to shore, above their knees in mud and water. Burne and I were carried ashore by a sailor!

They landed the heavy baggage first, and got most of it ashore, but when they were bringing our light baggage the wind was so high that they could not get it to land, and after beating about for more than an hour, they were obliged to go back to the vessel. So I had to sit in my wet things, but I do not think I am any the worse for it. Poor Murphy and Burne's servant were left on board the steamer all night, and had nothing to eat but a few biscuits. Four people called upon us and asked us to dinner. I agreed to go to the first, a retired Major, but when I could not get my things, I sent an excuse, but the Major sent up to say I was to go as I was. So I went in my surtout and blue trousers, and had a very pleasant evening. The barracks here are not finished, so the men are in billets, and we are at the inn, a miserable, dirty place. Burne has taken a small house and will be going in to it tomorrow, but I shall stay here, as I expect to return to Limerick when Captain James returns on 1st January. I like being with Burne very much, but I should like a little more time to myself. I cannot write when he is talking.

I hope you had a merry Christmas; it was a miserable one here. We could not get any beef, and nobody here has ever heard of a plum pudding. We were both anxious to have one, so I determined to make one. It was a fine large one, and would have been a very good one, if I had not put so much flour into it, and all the good things sank into one side of it, which we cut off. I rather liked it, and tried some of it cold yesterday, but Burne did not think much of it. The Knight of Glin (called that because he is the Head of a very old family) called upon us yesterday, and asked us to use his domain as we liked, and invited us to join a party for woodcock shooting. I borrowed a gun, but found there was neither powder nor shot to be got in this place, and Burne had only enough for himself. We dine with him tonight. He is a very rich man and Lieutenant for the County. The village and all the land about here belong to him.

Murphy was very pleased to see me again, and thought I was taller and stouter than before I was ill. The proclamation about arms was posted up here on Friday; they are all to be handed in by Wednesday. This is a very quiet part of the country.

This is rather a nice village, and in summer must be very pretty. There is a row of trees down each side of the street, which is a very wide one. I should be happy to remain here, but Burne is also anxious to stay, and as he is the Lieutenant I think they will let him. The people here are extremely civil and hospitable; they have all called upon us, and we were out dining again last night. The woodcock shooting was not very successful; the weather is not hard enough yet for there to be many birds. It was a great wonder nobody was shot. The old Knight was rather afraid, as he has been hit twice. He has a shot corn in his nose, close to his eye.

We had a very pleasant evening when we dined with him; a regular bachelors' party. It was through the Knight that we were sent here. He was afraid people might come from the disturbed areas and plunder his tenants, so he wrote to say he would resign his Commission of the Peace if troops were not sent. He lives in Glin Castle, a fine old building a short distance from the village and about 500 yards from the river, and from the river it looks very well indeed. It stands in a large demesne, which is very well wooded. He owns a lot of property but not as much as he used to. At one time he owned all the land from Tarbet to Limerick. His name is Fitzgerald but he is never called anything other than the Knight, and everyone addresses him as 'Knight', which sounds very odd, especially when we say "Good night, Knight". It is a very old title of which he is extremely proud, granted by Queen Elizabeth. There is only one other Knight in Ireland, the Knight of Kerry, who is the White Knight, while ours is the Green Knight. There was a Black Knight, but the title is extinct. I get on very comfortably with him. He is married with two sons and two daughters; his elder son and he do not speak. His two daughters married two brothers, and his elder son married the sister of these brothers.

We are the first detachment to come here for 20 years so we are a great sensation; the people stare at us as if we were some newly discovered wild animals. I have been almost devoured by fleas since I came here. There is a great line of Saints above my bed, and I hoped that they might guard me from the fleas, but they seem to have little regard for such folk in 1848. The people are very civil and many have called upon us with invitations."

Margaret sympathised with Harry; she remembered her experiences when she was following the 92nd, and stayed *"at poor village inns, with horrid insects on the blankets".*

Glin Castle, the ancestral home of one of the branches of the Fitzgerald family, which had played an important part in the history of Ireland for many centuries, had been built in 1780 and was a very elegant building. By the time Harry visited the Castle its external appearance had been altered by the addition of battlements and other ornamental features. It is still the home of the present Knight and Lady.

8th January 1848

"I hope we shall remain here for 5 or 6 months. So much moving about is very troublesome and expensive work; I have had quite enough of it lately, and have never

Glin Castle in Ireland, where Harry Loft was often entertained by the Knight of Glin.

Glin Castle from the River Shannon. The Castle is much as it was in Harry's time.

felt really settled since I rejoined until now. James is back, and looking better than I have ever seen him. He thinks that leaving such a pure air as Wexford to such an unhealthy place as Templemore was the reason that we both took the fever. I do not think the Knight of Glin is the hero of that work of Dr. Lever's for the person represented in it lived in Galway. I am glad to hear poor old Cureall is sold. I wish he had been directly after he won the Liverpool.

I heard from Faulk Allison the other day, who said that the Waites had a large party on Christmas Eve with a famous Christmas Tree. What is a Christmas Tree?

It is at last decided that I am to stay here. Burne left yesterday on the steamer for Limerick, which goes from Tarbet and calls here each morning. There is no pier so the passengers have to be taken out in a boat to meet it. We had both been anxiously waiting for word from HQ since we both wished to remain here. Burne thought that I should be ordered in, and he was in a dreadful state of mind when the order came for him to proceed as soon as possible, and I did what I could to console him."

Although Harry had considered Burne to be one of his best friends, and a very gentlemanly fellow, the strain of living in close proximity had produced some tension.

"I found it hard to get on with Burne all the time; he is a regular Irishman, and fancies he knows everything and can do everything better than anyone else, and that every thing he has is better than anyone else's. A little of him now and then is all very well, but to be obliged to hear him talk all day and every day is more than I could bear."

Harry felt very grand in a well-furnished establishment of his own, with only one drawback. Not surprisingly he had felt unsettled having to move his quarters seven times in the short time that he had been back with the Regiment.

13th January 1848

"I see from the paper that a greater depth of rain has fallen on Ireland during the last month than has ever been known; I can quite believe it. Yesterday was what James calls an insinuating day - you get wet without noticing it.

I have moved into the house that Burne took for 7 shillings a week. I have a bedroom and a sitting room and there is a kitchen and a small bedroom downstairs. There are three tables, six very stylish old-fashioned chairs, two presses, and no end of crockery. The only disagreeable thing is that the floor of my room is so thin that I can hear every word they say below, and Mrs. Murphy's children make such a noise. But it is much better than being in lodgings. If we stay here long I think I shall go upon the Irish plan of not paying rent, arming Murphy and defending the house against the landlord and the bailiffs."

Food was cheap, but Harry did not think much of the local butchers.

"One day I saw a poor half starved cow standing in a small very dirty yard. A few days afterwards Burne's servant came in to tell us that the butcher had only got some very poor meat. I said that perhaps it was the old cow I had seen in the yard, laughing

at the thought of such a thing, when to my horror the servant said, "Oh no, Sir. They pined that one for a week to make it tender, and you had a steak from it the day before yesterday." If they had pined it for two months I do not think it would have made any difference to it."

Although Glin itself was very quiet, it was feared there might be a general Irish uprising soon, and all the men were issued with extra ammunition, so that in future they were each to carry 90 rounds. There were always tales of unrest elsewhere.

"There was a man shot dead at Cashel this week, and the man who committed that murder at Ballybrophy was taken the other day. After the murder he enlisted in the 67th Regiment, and the police arrested him on parade in Cork. The special Commission at Limerick has acquitted very few of the prisoners. They have hung two and transported a great many. They have transported a very respectable farmer for life for concealing a murderer in his house, which will do a great deal of good."

Some crimes did not seem to be quite so overtly political.

"Mr. Waldron, a gentleman and a magistrate in Co. Roscommon, has been shot by the police. The Coroner had an order against him, and went to his house with some bailiffs and policemen to make a seizure. They found that a wall had been built all round the house to make it a fortress. As one of the bailiffs was breaking the gate, Mr. Waldron shot him. The police then fired at Mr. Waldron and killed him.

Poor Jopp died on Tuesday of pneumonia brought on by a neglected cold. He was a very nice fellow and only about 28. I went to see him just before we left Limerick, when he was at the house of his married sister. He bade me good-bye and said that as I was going on detachment we were not likely to see each other for some time. He little thought, poor fellow, that we never would. Canavan, who is a very old man who has risen from the ranks, will now get his Company. Mockler, who has been senior Ensign for a long time will get his Lieutenancy. I shall then have only two before me on the list, but one of them is not for purchase, which is unlucky for me.

I unfortunately dropped my watch some time since. I will have to send it to a watchmaker in Limerick. We have Murphy's watch hung on the wall, but its small hand is loose so it is impossible to know what o'clock it is. In fact I have not known the proper time within an hour or so for the last fortnight."

As well as being anxious about Harry's health, Margaret was also interested to discover whether his hair was growing again. *"Has it got the nice twist it used to have, or has the shaving made it come straight?"* Harry assured her; *"it is a very respectable length now at the sides, and is much longer at the back than I generally wear it and curls most fiercely. I shall have to let Murphy operate upon it soon, as there is no barber nearer than Limerick."*

17th January 1848

"Poor Jopp was buried on Saturday at Limerick. His remains were conveyed to

the Churchyard on a gun carriage drawn by four horses, the pall was supported by four of our Captains. Some of the officers and men of the 41st, 92nd, the Horse Artillery and the 1st Royal Dragoons attended, as well as ours. Jopp was a Freemason so three Limerick Lodges were there, as well as several private coaches. Our band and that of the 70th played the Dead March alternately. He had been 10 years in the service and is regretted by every one in the Regiment.

I let Murphy cut my hair and he did it very well. When Burne was here he wanted his hair cutting very much, so I offered to do it, and cut it in first rate style, but I had a pair of very poor scissors and in trying to cut a lock at the side of his head they unfortunately slipped and took a small piece out of his ear. Afterwards he offered to cut mine but there was a look in his eye which made me think it would be better to decline his offer.

I saw in a paper about three weeks since that a Mr. Jackson from near Louth made a bet that he could drive a pony only 12 hands high from somewhere near Louth to Grimsby, a distance of 17 miles, in an hour and a quarter. Have you heard anything about it?"

25th January 1848

"James, his wife and I dined with the Knight on Saturday to meet a Captain in the East India Company's Service, and had a very pleasant evening. The James' house is outside the village close to the river; mine is in the town and not nearly so nicely situated, but I have a good view of the river. As well as lodging money of six shillings a week, I get 2s 8d for fuel. As you will remember, dear Mama, they burn nothing but turf here, and it is very cheap. Altogether I do not lose much by there being no barracks. I was weighed and measured on my birthday. I was 6 feet in my boots, and weighed 11st.13lbs. which is 4lbs. lighter than on my last birthday.

We all wore black crape on our arms for a month after Jopp's funeral. If we stay here until the Regiment leaves Limerick, I shall have to go in to collect things, so shall call on Major Thorold and Captain Sutherland. The 92nd was inspected in the New Barracks soon after they came to Limerick, and as the Colonel was on leave Major Thorold (who is a capital drill) put them through a great many movements. The men did everything beautifully and were much admired. They certainly are very fine fellows, and cut us out altogether."

3rd February 1848

"The retired Major, with whom I dined on the day I arrived, offered to lend me a gun whenever I liked, so as James was going out today I borrowed the gun and went with him. We found plenty of snipe but missed a great number of them. In the end I got six and James got three. We have had some sharp frosts, and the gentlemen round here are busy filling their ice-houses. Cartloads of ice are brought in from the country. Great numbers of salmon are caught here in the season, which are sent off

at once to London and other places. They are put in boxes and packed in the ice, broken up into small pieces, to keep them fresh. The way the salmon are caught is by having a row of upright poles running out a good long way into the river, and to these a net is fixed. The fish is stopped by the net and swims along the line of poles till he comes to an opening which has been left on purpose. He fancies this is the way out but finds himself fast in the net. The season commenced yesterday. I was invited by the Knight to join in shooting his covers last week, but I had no powder or shot and none is to be found nearer than Tarbet. They killed eight brace of woodcock.

A gentleman here, who has been living in great style, lately got into difficulties, and the other day a bailiff came with a writ against him, but the gentleman escaped and his servants made the bailiff eat his writ. The bailiffs then moved into the house in force, and the gentleman and his wife are hiding somewhere in Limerick. While the Commission has been sitting, several houses have been attacked in this county in the last fortnight by armed men with their faces blackened, who demanded money to hire counsel for the defence of the prisoners, though it is said they want the money to hire men to pick off a few jurymen and witnesses.

It is said that we are soon to be relieved by a Company of the 92nd, but I hope it is not so, as I like this place very much and have no desire to go back into Limerick. I got rid of my cough about a week ago but I caught cold again the other day somehow or other. One of our men killed himself at Rathkeale the other day by drinking a bottle of whiskey at a draught."

9th February 1848

"I dined with the Knight on Sunday. There were only four of us; the Knight, his wife (who is addressed as 'Lady'), and his cousin, the retired Major. I have had a bit of a cold for some time, and recently a bowel complaint. I took some calomel and some pills, but they did me no good. I then took some castor oil, which did me a little good, but in a few days I was as bad as ever, so I took some more last Wednesday and am now rather better. I spent my birthday by myself, 'playing at nothing with nobody' as Jem says.

Murphy has got an absurd idea into his head that this house is haunted. He says he and his wife have several times heard footsteps crossing the floor of my sitting room, and the door shutting, and that he is sure they are not the footsteps of a living being!

On Sundays I march the Roman Catholics to the chapel at a quarter to nine, and then we have our own service at noon in the church, which is built in the Knight's domain, and is rather a nice-looking building, bit it is cold and damp."

Life at Glin suited Harry very well.

"Food is still cheap. I bought a couple of very fine live geese today for 2/6d. I only wear uniform on special occasions. I go about in the same dress as I used to wear at Healing, which is quite good enough for this place. Even when the Knight

invites me to dinner, he always says I am not to make a dandy of myself but to come in a shooting jacket or any old thing. I have never got to know so many people on detachment before, or had so many invitations to dine and shoot. I get on very well with James who is very good about inviting me to their house, and going shooting with me. He says he will never forgive me, because he missed a couple of snipe and I wiped his eye and got them both with a right and left."

15th February 1848

"I was most disappointed to learn today that the route has come for our departure to Ballingarry on Thursday, to relieve one of our other Companies. It is a village about 9 miles from Croome. Mr Fitzgerald, the clergyman at Tarbet, has invited me to dinner tomorrow, but with all the packing to be done in so short a time I shall not be able to go. I am better than I was but not quite well yet. If I am no better when I get to Ballingarry I will consult someone. I think I am thinner than I was, and those places have been discharging a good deal, and one of them is a little painful."

18th January 1848

Margaret was always concerned about Harry's health, and one of her letters at this time gives some indication of her concern and the reason for it.

"I am so thankful that there is no consumption in the Loft family or in ours. For although your poor Papa was carried off by consumption, it was entirely caused by circumstances and neglect, as all the medical men agreed that from his breadth of chest there was no tendency to that complaint, and they all said that there could not be a finer constitution than he had; but he was very incautious in exposing himself to the heavy dews that are so dangerous in the West Indies.

After a most severe attack of Yellow Fever, he came to Edinburgh Castle, a most cold and exposed situation; a very great change. But he thought nothing of that, and used to go about with a thin jacket, and no Flannel at all. When they played football or cricket, or feats of leaping or throwing the shot, he wore no jacket at all. Whilst we were in Ireland he was equally careless of himself in spite of everything I could say. He had a very bad cold, for which he was being given medicine, but still went out hunting. They had a very hard run but he stood about afterwards in the damp, so his cold got worse and he had an attack of inflammation of the lung. Before he was better, although the Doctor offered to give him a certificate to that effect, he went out still-hunting at nights. The poor fellow seemed to forget how much he had been tried, and so the small pox attacked his most delicate parts. Even after we came to England, the poor dear fellow went out on long shooting expeditions with Mr. Smyth at Elkington, rode and leaped a horse nobody else could do anything with - in short acted in a way no invalid should have, and sadly was carried off before his 26th birthday."

'Still-hunting' meant going out into the country to find and destroy illicit stills for making poteen. One such expedition in which Thomas took part was on the evening of St. Patrick's Day, when it was thought that those involved in the illegal activity would be more interested in drinking their product than in making it, and so would be at their least alert.

Glin had been a place where Harry had obviously been happier than in any other of his postings. Ballingarry was not going to replace it in his affections.

The colonisation of Ireland by England

CHAPTER 7
ON DETACHMENT AGAIN

Harry, as usual, gave a full account of the Company's march to their new station. His first impression of Ballingarry was not very encouraging. The two recurring subjects in his letters now were his health and his chance of promotion, since he was now reaching the top of the Ensigns' list. He knew that it was impossible for him to raise enough money to purchase his 'step', so that his promotion depended upon succeeding a Lieutenant whose commission was 'not for purchase'.

22nd February 1848

"I went out shooting on Wednesday because James wanted a couple of 'cocks' to send to someone. The Knight's son and his agent, Mr. Parker, a crack shot, were with us. We only got 2½ couple, so James had one over. I got in at 3 o'clock, and Murphy and I had everything ready for weighing by 5. A Company of the 41st arrived by the steamer to take over from us. On Thursday I had a good breakfast at the hotel and we started marching at ten o'clock. It was rather tiring over the mountains. We did about 15 miles along an absurdly twisting road to Newcastle. Before we got there we met Bailey, a young fellow of the 88th (the Connaught Rangers), on horseback, who asked James and me to dine at their mess. He offered several times to let one of us ride, but we preferred walking. We went to the Barracks and found that luncheon was all ready for us. Then they brought us socks and slippers so we could change out of our boots, and sit comfortably through the afternoon.

We dined at seven with two officers of the 88th, an officer of the 1st Dragoons, and a Poor Law Commissioner who used to be in the Army. The Rangers Captain had his right eye knocked out by a racket ball, so he is learning to shoot from his left shoulder. Bailey is the man we had heard of who was said to have jumped his horse over the mess table at Tralee. When one of the others said they did not believe it, Bailey had his mare brought in, and after refusing twice the mare cleared it beautifully, sailing between the branches of the large candle-stick!

We were late starting the next morning because the Sergeants could not get the men together, and they did not step out well because they had had a hard march the day before, and had not had any breakfast. We reached Ballingarry after a march of 9 miles. James did not march with us, but came on afterwards in a car. Ballingarry is the most miserable, dirty, horrid place I have ever seen. The men are quartered in wretched barracks which are part of an old castle, and there are no decent lodgings for James and me. James has sent a letter to the General stating that the barracks are not at all satisfactory, and should not be used in this state.

My cough is pretty much the same. I have had it quite long enough. At all the detachments there is a Dr. Surgeon appointed to look after the officers and men. I intend to speak to him today. If we go to India we shall have two Lieutenant-Colonels, which will give another step, and the Senior Ensign will get his Lieutenancy.

Captain Sutherland called on me yesterday. He walked over from Castletown with his Sub. who is called Duff, I think. I guessed who he was directly I saw him. After their visit I walked some of the way back with them. They showed me the easiest way to Castletown and asked me to come over any day when I had nothing else to do. I liked him very much; he is a nice amusing fellow. He enquired very kindly after you, dear Mama, and begged to be remembered to you most kindly, even though he did not deserve it, as he is such a bad correspondent. He also asked after Aunt Christina. I have done as you suggested and burned 100 letters, because they are such a trouble to carry round with me. Of course, dear mama, I will always keep the ones from you and Jem. I have got my watch back. It cost 7s. 6d."

Robert Macleod Sutherland had joined the 92nd in 1825, at the same time as Thomas Loft, so he had already served for 23 years when Harry met him. He had been the only person to know about Thomas's secret engagement to Margaret. Margaret was delighted to hear about his visit to Harry. *"He was always such a nice fellow, and by your account has not changed. He was a very good friend to your dear Father, and will I am sure be an equally good friend to you. He was very fond of sport, though I think fishing was his favourite amusement."*

There were other memories that returned to Margaret. She was anxious to find out if their old servant, Mylne, was still in the 92nd. "A black looking fellow in No. 8 Company. Many an hour has he nursed you on his knee, and sung you to sleep. I am sure he would be delighted to see you, if he is still with the Regiment."

It is doubtful if Ensign Loft would have been as delighted by such an encounter as Private Mylne. When Harry mentioned that the Bands of the 92nd and the 64th had been playing at a Ball in Limerick, she wrote: *"How much I should love to hear them play 'Hey, Johnny Cope' again. It is still the Regimental March, is it not?"*

Sutherland eventually reached the rank of Colonel.

29th February 1848

"I saw the Doctor yesterday; who gave me some medicine, and said I should remain in the house as much as possible. He saw me again today and said I should go on the sick list for a few days and not go out at all. He is going to put a blister on me tonight, and I am not to have any meat at all, which I do not like the idea of at all. He tried my chest with his stethoscope and said it was all right. I spoke to him about the boils, and he said they were rather beneficial than otherwise, but I shall speak to him again about them, because one of them is very troublesome. I have had some list nailed on my door to make it more comfortable. There is no sentry box here, so when it rains the sentry has to stand in the hall with the door open, which makes the house very cold and draughty."

Margaret had just agreed to have a young man as a lodger. *"Mr. Swan, a very wealthy attorney and a gentleman of good family, has persuaded me to take his son as a lodger. John is between 16 and 17, and is coming into Mr. Allison's office as an Articled Clerk. He will be company for Jem, and should enable me to save a little money towards Jem's college expenses. He is taller than Jem - a nice looking youth and would have been handsome but for a hare lip, which has been sewn, but still misfigures him. His mother told me that her son was 'of a very obliging disposition, steady, quiet, and cheerful. On the whole he has good health but is of a rather languid constitution, and I should be obliged if you would remind him of the necessity of taking regular exercise and rising early. Plain food suits him best. He requires meat twice a day at breakfast and dinner'."*

This meant finding a bigger house than the one in Lee Street, where she and the boys had lived since they left Elkington.

"I have had great difficulty in finding a house to suit me, as we must have four bedrooms. Mrs. Eleanor Philbrick's I should have liked, as it looks into a great garden, but it is too small. Mrs. Kerr's in Westgate would have done, but a cellar kitchen is a great nuisance when you only have one servant. Moreover it is in a very forlorn state, for it was made quite an Irish cabin of by poor Mr. Neill. I have decided upon one of four or five large ones at the back of the Prison, not a great way from the Station. I should have preferred a house more in the town, though I certainly prefer this to being shut up in one of the close streets. There is that large field on the west side, and it is nice and open towards the railway, so we shall have plenty of fresh air and no lime smoke. (There was a lime quarry and kiln at the top of Lee Street, not far from their former house). *The windows look over the Prison gardens; the front room is a good deal raised above the street, with iron railings in front. Altogether a good respectable looking house. Jem thinks it will be noisy, but I think it will be rather amusing to see all the people and vehicles passing to the Station."*

5th March 1848

"Odell, the Surgeon of the Bays, was in town and the Doctor asked him to have a look at me. He seemed to think my chest was quite satisfactory. I told him I was very hot in the night, and sometimes woke in a proper lather. I hope you will be comfortable with young Swann. I should think the house you speak of is a very nice one, and will be much better than one in the town. I do not like that part of the town as much as where we live now. It will be a great advantage having two sitting rooms. I am glad that Uncle Wallis is to be buried in England. He was always very kind to us."

Uncle Wallis was James Wallis Loft, Harry's godfather. He had been living with his wife in Paris, having been forced to leave England because of his scandalous behaviour with Mrs. Smyth of Elkington. He had died very suddenly, and after a series of complicated arrangements his body was brought to Hull by sea, and then carried from New Holland to North Thoresby on the railway, which had only been opened ten days previously. The final stage was by hearse from Thoresby to Marshchapel, where several generations of his ancestors had been buried.

"The clergyman here invited me to tea on Friday night. It was a small party; just James and Mrs. J. and another clergyman and his wife from Limerick. We had a regular tea shine, and then a good deal of music. Altogether it was a pleasant evening. Captain Sutherland is a red-faced, good-tempered looking fellow, with very short light hair. He looks quite 40.

Captain Sutherland has been over to see me again in the pouring rain. As he had to walk back to Castletown he thought it prudent not to sit too long. It was a curious day for anyone to go out walking, but he said he had to come in to town any way, and he was tired of sitting in the house. The weather continues to be as bad as ever. I think it has rained every day since we came here."

14th March 1848

"I have had two blisters on my chest. It is rather better but not inclined to go away completely. I am anxious to get well again as soon as I can, as James told me he should have to report me to HQ before the 17th, as if they found out that I had been on the sick list so long he might get into a row. He has been doing all the duty while I have been ill, and sits with me for a short time every day. Is that not good of him? I did not feel the first blister at all, but the second was very painful and I was awake nearly all night. There was a great discharge from it all yesterday. I had quite enough of Mr. Murphy's method of dressing a blister at Templemore, so I always take them off myself, as I can get at them this time. The Doctor gave me ointment for the boils.

Captain Sutherland and Duff came to visit me yesterday, and while they were here the clergyman, Mr. Gubbins (not a very pretty name, is it?) came in. I should say he is on the wrong side of 40, is married and has 7 or 8 children.

You have probably seen in the paper that there are to be meetings in every parish in Ireland on St. Patrick's Day to get up a petition for the repeal of the Union. There are bills and stickers about one to be held here in the Chapel yard, and the priest gave it out in the Chapel on Sunday."

19th March 1848

"I do not think the second blister has done me much good, though I cough less now, except in the morning when I first awake. The boils do not pain me, but if they are going they are going very slowly. The Colonel has told James that I shall be relieved in a short time, so I expect to go into Limerick soon. We heard today that poor Smith, who has been on sick leave since last May, is dead and Bowlby has got his Lieutenancy. Canavan sent in his papers some time since, and Du Cane will soon be a Lieutenant, so that I shall then be Senior Ensign. If I had been able to purchase

I should have got my Lieutenancy now. Littleton is going to sell, and Thompson will go over my head, which is a great nuisance. There was no meeting here last Friday. A band was playing up and down the town but only about 3 or 4 people followed it. They are going to try again next week, but the Magistrates do not expect any disturbance, though there might be if we were not here. Sutherland has been over twice since I last wrote, but he only stays a short time.

Last Monday The Assistant Adjutant-General sent to James to know how long it would be before I was fit for duty, so he got a certificate from the Doctor, stating that it would be some time, and that he recommended me to get leave. On Wednesday Shute appeared as my relief, with orders for me to report at Limerick. James and Mrs. J. were very kind, and discovered that the only covered car in Ballingarry belonged to Mr. Cox, and unfortunately he was using it to go to the sale of the house at Glin where the servants had been so polite to the bailiff! So James walked over to Rathkeale and got me a covered car there. It was a very long, cold and tiring journey, but the jolting of the car kept me warm. I had some luncheon at Adare, and reached Limerick at 6.30 pm, where the Colonel said I did not look very ill, and Carter got me a room for the night. The next day he arranged a very fine room for me, a great improvement on the one at Ballingarry. Poor Shute could not believe his eyes when he saw what a wretched place he would have to live in.

I saw Smith, (the Regimental Surgeon) today, who said there is no necessity for me to go on leave, unless the cough does not get better soon, as he hopes the change of air from Ballingarry to this place will do me good."

26th March 1848

"Today Smith made another change in my diet. He lets me have eggs and some soup in the middle of the day, instead of milk and arrowroot. My chest has been rubbed all over with ointment and is covered with spots which are very troublesome. I am inhaling steam every morning, which Smith says will make me expectorate. He would not give me an answer about getting leave, and it would go against me having had leave a short time ago, but if the cough persists he will recommend me to a warmer climate. I hope, dear Mama, you will not write to anybody in the Regiment about me, as if you did I should never hear the last of it. It is a good thing that my room looks over the square, so I can see everything that happens."

9th April 1848

"I am still having soup, rice and tea, so you may imagine I am not looking very stout. Smith has just come in to say he will recommend me for two months leave, but that I must go to Bath because he says Lincolnshire is too cold for me. But I shall not stay at Bath very long! How I reckon of seeing poor old Louth again!

There is much talk of a rising in Dublin shortly, and that the people are busy making an immense number of pikes. All our Companies have been issued with an extra 30 rounds per man, and a third of each detachment and one officer must always be in barracks."

Without informing Harry, Margaret had been writing to Captain James's wife in an attempt to find out more about Harry's condition. She was relieved when he put himself under the care of the local medical man at Ballingarry, but she had no great confidence in him, and was pleased when Dr. Odell, the Cavalry Surgeon in the district, was called in, and pronounced that Harry's lungs were as sound as a bell, which would seem to have been a rather optimistic diagnosis.

Margaret wrote on the subject of his night sweats; *"You have always perspired a great deal during the night all your life, and all the Loft family do. You might just mention this to the Doctor. You could also tell the medical man that the Doctor here, who had you in his charge while you had Fever, says that at your age the boils are an effect of nature and a relief to the constitution, and so should not be checked."*

She also advocated the use of medicated cotton:

"Mrs. Sooby, who has just returned from London, tells me it is very much used and recommended by all the faculty there, after Influenza and when there is any delicacy of the chest. It is the very best preservative against the effects of these trying easterly winds. It is something like wadding, and is sewed inside the flannel waistcoat."

Margaret began to urge Harry to apply for sick leave, as she was most uncomfortable at the thought of him being alone in his room for so long, with so much pain, and living on a very low diet. She certainly had considered writing to the Colonel of the 64th, and even to General Sir John Macdonald, who had commanded the 92nd in her husband's time, to get their support for Harry's application for leave, but thought better of it, which was just as well for Harry's peace of mind. She thought she would be able to borrow a 'respirator' for him from Dr. Banks, her doctor at Louth, as she thought it was imperative that he had one, before he undertook the journey. She also sent him 'a Bill of the Railway' with the times of trains between New Holland and Louth on the newly opened railway.

Mrs. James had continued to keep Margaret informed of Harry's condition and on 7th April sent her a copy of the report of Dr. Smith, Surgeon to the 64th, which was much less optimistic than the impression he was giving to Harry about his condition. It stated:

"I am sorry to say that I do not consider Mr. Loft's state of health at all favourable, the affection of his chest being now of considerable duration. Altho' he has had no return of the pain in his chest, yet a hard dry cough, hurried respiration on the slightest exertion and almost nightly fever continues. This leads me to think that considerable mischief has taken place in his lungs. He is however better than when he came here, and I hope the warmer weather may aid him."

12th April 1848

"I have got my leave and start tomorrow morning for Cork. I shall stay the night there, and then sail on Friday for Bristol. I do not know when we arrive there, but I believe it is rather a long passage. I do not much like the idea of going to Bath, but you may be sure, dear Mama, I shall not stay there long."

At the same time as Harry was writing this Dr. Smith was sending another report to Margaret, even more alarming than his first one. *"I cannot conceal from you that he has a strong tendency to serious pulmonary disease, and I would thoroughly recommend his removal to India, the climate of which is warm, dry, and equable, and where chest affections are almost unknown. I was threatened in the same way many years ago, and went to the East in consequence, where I got well immediately, and had no return during the seven years I was there. In your son's case I dread the coming autumn in England, and would strenuously advise, should his symptoms become mitigated shortly, that an application should be made to have him transferred to a Corps on the Indian establishment. The climate in Ireland is very unsuitable for people with chest disease, owing to its variableness and dampness."*

On 13th April Harry left Limerick and crossed from Cork to Bristol where Uncle Fred met him. They travelled by train to Bath, where Fred was due to be married in a few weeks time to Gloriana Saunders, the daughter of Rear-Admiral James Saunders and his wife Ann, who was a niece of John Loudon MacAdam, the originator of the macadam system of road-building.

17th April 1848

"I feel very well and not at all knocked up by the journey. Uncle advised me to call in Dr. Boie, who seems to know what he is about. He allows me an egg to my breakfast, and some chops and a glass of beer at 1.30 pm, so there is no fear of my getting so weak again. I think my cough is not as hard as it was before the voyage. Uncle has got me some very nice lodgings, and runs about for everything I want. Miss MacAdam (the aunt of Gloriana Saunders) *has kindly offered me her carriage today, and Uncle has gone to fetch it so that we can have a drive."*

Gloriana wrote an encouraging letter to Margaret about Harry's condition and the way in which he had borne the long voyage. She had been largely instrumental in finding the comfortable lodgings for Harry, and Alfred had taken a room in the same house in order to be able to look after him, since he was so grateful for the way in which Harry had assisted him during his illness in Ireland. *"Since it is very near us I trust we may be able to make his time pass tolerably for him."* However, in spite of the Surgeon's advice against Harry going to Lincolnshire as its climate would be too severe, whereas Bath was considered entirely healthy and beneficial to invalids, on 12th May Harry was in Hull, where Margaret was staying with the Lundies. By 19th

May they were back in Louth, travelling from Grimsby to Louth on the railway which had been opened two months previously. The journey took a quarter of the time which the tide-coaches had taken. Harry saw their new house in Ramsgate for the first time.

Harry's convalescence this time was a very protracted affair, and it was obvious to many of his friends that his future was uncertain. With Dr. Smith's words constantly in her mind Margaret must have been very worried, but managed, as usual, to make the best of things, and tried to ensure that he was well cared for, and able to enjoy all his old pursuits as far as possible. Both of them got a lot of pleasure in driving out in a gig lent by Mr. Sutton, one of their neighbours, which resulted in various adventures without causing it or them any permanent damage. Neither of them was an accomplished whip, but each thought they were better than the other.

A round of visits was made to their friends and relations, and towards the end of the year Harry spent some time at Stewton House, the new and splendid home of the Banks family, so that the Doctor could make a prolonged observation of his case, and decide whether he was fit to rejoin his Regiment. The Doctor had always been eager for his elder son, Charley, to be in Harry's company as much as possible since he considered him to be a good influence, unlike some of Charley's other friends.

Margaret, Harry and James, as they had often done in previous years, spent a very cheerful Christmas at Binbrook Hill, the home of the Iles family where they enjoyed all the usual events, the musical parties and the Quadrille evenings, shooting and hunting. To have a fire in her bedroom was a luxury for Margaret, and most evenings ended with her and the motherless Iles sisters sitting round it, having a good gossip.

Harry was informed that the 64th was under orders for India, and would sail from Cork in the beginning of 1849. The Depot was to be set up at Chatham, and it was assumed at Headquarters that Harry would be stationed there. Although there were still doubts about the effect of the voyage and the Indian climate on Harry's health, Doctor Banks eventually concluded that Harry would probably benefit from the long voyage, and suggested that he tried to get his posting changed. Time was short if the necessary arrangements were to be made, both with the Regiment and also for Harry's personal requirements, since he would need new kit for the tropics, and the 64th had finally decided to wear shell jackets, and sling sword belts instead of frog ones. To his great joy he was gazetted Lieutenant on 22nd December, without purchase, so he would also need new badges of rank.

He and Margaret went to London on 29th December to see to all this, travelling by train the whole way, since the railway line to King's Cross was now complete. Margaret stayed with her sister, Christina Kilner, in Islington, but little Martin Kilner had just died and Harry had lodgings over a nearby baker's shop. The warmth of the oven was very comforting to Harry, as the weather was bitterly cold, and in future the smell of newly baked bread was to be a constant reminder to Margaret of these few, very hectic, days. Harry had been advised that many items of equipment could be bought more cheaply in India, but some things were not available there, notably a saddle and bridle, which had to be bought in London.

Harry had never had "a likeness" made, so Margaret decided they would have Harry's portrait painted. It happened that while she was living in Edinburgh, before her marriage, a family called Bell were next-door neighbours to her great friends the Campbells. In spite of family opposition from the Campbells, John Zephanaiah Bell, an artist, married Jane Campbell. He later established himself in London as a painter, particularly of classical landscapes. So Margaret, with her usual readiness to pull strings on her sons' behalf, got in touch with Jane, and arranged that Zephanaiah would paint a full-length portrait of Harry in his uniform. It was possible to have only three sittings, and the new uniform with Lieutenant's badges was only available for the third one. One of Margaret's vivid memories of this time was of the long walk, in bitter cold weather, from Bell's studio in Seymour Street, along Piccadilly and the Strand, back to Islington, after the last sitting.

Harry was in constant touch with the Regiment, and there was still doubt about his future. The Regiment was now in Cork, almost ready for embarkation, and the Depot was about to be set up. At the last minute the decision was made, and on 6th January 1849 he caught the 10.15 am train from Paddington to Bristol. In fact he nearly missed the train because of *"a very careful cabbie."* By 3.30 pm he was on the Cork packet. During the crossing he met Dr. Archer, the new Surgeon to the 64th, who had exchanged with the former Surgeon, Dr. Smith, and also Lieutenant MacRae of the 64th, who was under orders for India but was very anxious to stay in England. There is a suggestion that MacRae would not in any case have been permitted to leave England because of the large debts he had accumulated. It was agreed that the two Lieutenants would request to exchange postings, and a hurried visit was paid to the Colonel and application made to the General. Dr. Archer provided a certificate in which he stated that he thought Harry would benefit from the posting and the voyage out.

12th January 1849

"The Colonel got an answer today, and I am to go. I feel very much at leaving you all, but I think it is the best to go at once, as I have to go some time. I could not have remained in the army to serve in this country. It is impossible to do the duty and to look after yourself properly; having to go out in all weathers. I hope our vessel will not be long getting here. It is miserable work here at present. As the vessels are ordered not to touch anywhere except at the Cape, if the wind is favourable, I thought it better to get a dozen more shirts. They are very nice ones, 2/6d each. I have also got 6 more flannel shirts and 6 pairs of drawers. I was on a Court Martial on Monday and on Guard on Tuesday."

This was a rather uncomfortable period, of the sort which has been familiar to soldiers throughout the ages. *"Everything is bustle and confusion".* It rained continually. The town was crowded because the 70th and the 83rd Regiments were also waiting to embark. All the gear was packed, some of the ships had already sailed, there was no Mess, and so Harry was sleeping in the Imperial Hotel. Everybody was hanging about aimlessly, waiting for the troopships. Inevitably there was a stream of conflicting rumours about what had happened to the ships on their passage from Falmouth, involving dismasting, total wreck, and mutiny. Regimental Headquarters, under Colonel Stopford, was to sail on the 'Java', one division under Captain James, who had now obtained command of the elite Grenadier Company, was to sail on the 'John Brewer', another on the 'Tulloch Castle' and the remainder, including Harry's Company, now commanded by Captain Bingham, was to sail on 'The Earl of Balcarres' under Major Western. All the ships belonged to the East India Company.

19th January 1849

"I have been wonderfully well, considering everything. My cough is better than it was in London, and I have been raising very little lately. I felt my pulse this morning and it was 86. I find I have not to advance the Captain of the vessel anything. We are allowed 4/- a day for our messing by government, from which the Captain finds our breakfasts, dinners, etc. It has been expensive living here, and I shall need some ready money when we get there, to buy a tent, bullocks and other things. Twemlow, Fanning, Alexander and myself usually dine together. I like Twemlow very much. He came to us from the 4th, and has been in India, which he says is a delightful country and a good climate, if a person only takes common care of himself. Fanning, who is in Bingham's Company with me, is a good-tempered and amusing Irishman. He was in Tobago with the 1st West Indian Regiment for some time, but he does not remember Uncle Willie's name. Alexander is the smallest officer I ever saw. He is about the same height as Henry Iles, but nothing like as stout, and I do not think he will grow any more. At first sight you would guess his age to be between 13 and 16, but he is 19, I think. It is quite absurd to see him in his regimentals, and like all small men he is dreadfully conceited. I did not see much of Hood, the man from Lincoln, because he has already embarked on the Tulloch Castle. It sailed first and the Java, with our HQ, and the Bombay, with that of the 83rd, sailed yesterday. There will be a regular race between them, because there is a bet between the Captains about which will reach Bombay first. I hope it will be the Java, as it makes a great deal of difference when we are coming home. If one regiment lands only an hour before another, it will be the first to come home. We get double pay too, as soon as HQ land.

I saw Murphy the other day, who wanted to know if I was going out. He is not doing so, as he is not fit for anything but being a servant. He was servant to James when I left, and now he is with Cumberlidge. I should have liked to have old Murphy again, for he is a capital fellow. I am glad he has got a good master. There was no chance of me having the wings (The Grenadier Company wore special wings on the shoulders of their jackets) *but if I could have had a choice of Companies, putting James's out of the way, I should have chosen Bingham's so I am very lucky. He is a friendly gentlemanly fellow, and a good officer. I do not know Grylls, our sub. well, but he seems a good-natured fellow, though he has not much to say for himself. I think that answers all your questions."*

25th January 1849

"Cork is a good large place, but dirty of course. It is built in a complete hole. The barracks are quite outside up a tremendous hill. The countryside is very pretty, and we get capital views down the river. It is as nice a place as any I have seen in Ireland, but I shall be glad to leave it. I cough very little and do not raise much in the morning. I had a little pain in my chest. I put on a couple of turpentine plaisters when the pain was bad, and I have not felt anything of it since. I have not been taking the oil, but I will do so as soon as I get on board the ship. My appetite is very good and I enjoy my meals more than ever. I drink porter and altogether am taking as much care of myself as possible, but I don't think I should ever get rid of my cough in this country, even though it is so much warmer than England.

I have been wearing my new shell jacket, and do not find it at all cold, because the weather here may be wet, but it is much warmer than London. They look much better than I expected, at least ours do. I think they look very neat, but with yellow facings and cuffs they are horrible. I am glad to find I shall be able to wear my old blue coat on ship. We shall dine in our jackets with black waistcoats, as it would be impossible to wear white ones on board. We do not wear the sash with our jackets. I do not like the new sling sword-belt much, as it does not do to be trailing it always behind you, or carrying it in your hand, and when it is hooked up it does not carry as nicely as the old frog belt (The sling sword-belt is still in the possession of Harry's family). *All the other ships have sailed now, except for the John Brewer, but the Earl of Balcarres is such a fast sailer we may be there as soon as any of them. We shall share her with 85 men and two Ensigns of the 83rd. I now find that it costs £100; we have to pay the Captain £5 and the Government pays the other £95."*

Harry whiled away some of the time by reading a copy of the account written by Peter Martin, Margaret's brother, who had sailed for India to join the East India Company's army in 1829, just twenty years previously, which interested him very much. There was a General Inspection of all the troops in Cork by General Turner.

31st January 1849

"We were all drawn up on three sides of the barracks square. It was a pretty sight, but the weather was wretched, so the General did not bother us much, once he had inspected the ranks, and we had marched past in slow and quick time, and then

we were dismissed. The 12th Lancers looked very well, but I do not much like their uniform; all blue, with red facings, which makes them look too much like artillerymen. It is wonderful how well their horses are trained."

There was further delay, during which time Harry visited *HMS Ganges*, a 2nd rate of 84 guns built in Bombay in 1821.

"She was lying about ½ mile off. The officers were very civil and offered us a glass of wine, and showed us all over. She is a most beautiful vessel. You cannot imagine how clean everything was. She has a complement of 750 men. They told us that the Balcarres, which is nearly as large as Ganges, is a splendid sailer and one of the largest merchantmen in the world. She was built in 1815 and weighs 1,800 tons. With a fair wind we could get to Bombay in three months."

In 1865 *The Ganges* became a training ship, and survived until 1929, giving its name to the Royal Naval shore training establishment at Ipswich, familiar to several generations of seamen.

The Earl of Balcarres finally sailed from Cove on 11th February 1849, the last of the troopships to leave for India.

The Earl of Balcarres, the East India Company ship in which Harry sailed to India.

CHAPTER 8

TO INDIA

Harry found life on board *The Earl of Balcarres* very strange to begin with. At the start of the voyage to India he was able to send a letter home by the pilot cutter with some details.

January 1849

"We were brought out to the ship in a small steamer. I have a capital cabin, 11 feet by 9. It has a large port, which will be very nice in the hot weather, but at present the cabin is very cold, for during the day I have to keep the port open, as there is only a small bull's eye in the deadlight, and the cabin is very dark. I can stand up comfortably in it, except where there are three large beams. I have got everything put to rights, and am very comfortable. I have had a wash hand stand made in one corner of the cabin, with hooks put up for my cot and swing tray, and all my things fastened down; my drawers in their chests, my tub, my portmanteau, and bullock trunk. There is a large earthenware jug for fresh water, which is given out every day. My cot is taken down every morning and put to one side; then I put the mattress on the drawer chest where it makes a kind of sofa.

The Balcarres is a most splendid vessel, and the Captain is a good sort of fellow, much more of a gentleman than these skippers usually are. We have a cow on board and an immense number of hens, turkeys and other poultry. We shall have fresh meat all the way. We breakfast at 9 am, then there are spirits and biscuits on the table at noon, dinner at 4 pm, tea at 8 pm, and spirits again at 9, so I think we do pretty well. There is claret and port and sherry every day, and champagne on Sundays and Thursdays.

We were delayed in sailing, because eight of the seamen refused to work, and were put ashore and got three months imprisonment. Fortunately the Captain was able to procure replacements. We have an orderly officer every day, and have to take watches day and night, but there are nine subs so that it does not come round very often. I was on last night from 8 till 12, and shall be on again tomorrow from 4 till 8. I shall like it very well when the weather warms, but it is cold work at present. The Major read Prayers this morning.

All our Surgeons have embarked, but there is a Doctor appointed to the Balcarres, a Scotchman. I don't know how we shall all get on, as we have a great many different characters, and four months is a long time to be fastened up together. I expect the women will quarrel like bricks before we have been very long at sea.

Fanning is a very amusing fellow, and I like him. He was very anxious to have some badger baiting before we sailed, and ordered a man from the town to bring up a badger, but he did not come till too late. Fanning is taking his bull dogs out with him. They are regular devils, which will go in at anything. He has chalked 'Beware of the Bull dogs' over his cabin door, and they should certainly keep his possessions safe.

The fellows all think I look too well to have been really ill. Jeffery came up the other day and said, 'Here's Loft fairly bursting with rude health. I should not much like to meet him on a dark night'. I was weighed the other day, and am now 12 stone."

During the voyage to India *The Earl of Balcarres* was never in sight of land after the first day at sea. So there was no opportunity of sending letters home until they reached their destination. Harry was seasick for the first three days, but never felt ill for the rest of the voyage. He did not keep a journal of the voyage, so the only account of it is a rather concise one, without any mention of his fellow passengers or of the daily routine on the ship that he wrote to Margaret when they had reached India. He took a long time over writing the letter, which included this account, so the chronology is sometimes a little uncertain.

7th June 1849

"For some time after we left Ireland the weather was bad and somehow I caught cold, but I put on a blister and kept it open for a few days, and did not eat any meat, and by the time we got near the Line I was all right again. We crossed the Line in Longitude 25° on 12th March at 8 o'clock at night, when Neptune hailed us and then came on board and made a speech. The Captain gave him some grog, and he was drawn away on his car by four bears. They threw some lighted tar barrels overboard, which looked very well, dancing over the waves. There was no shaving or anything of that kind, because the Captain would not allow it, as none of us liked the idea of being shaved and ducked by rascally sailors.

A few days later we spoke to the Fanny, a ship bound for Liverpool from Rio di Janeiro. I had a long letter for you, but when I came up on deck with it I found the Captain had already sent a boat across. I was very annoyed. We never saw another ship.

We rounded the Cape on 12th April and went as far as 40 degrees south in order to make our Easting. It was most fearfully cold and there was a tremendous gale, so we ran along that latitude making 1,000 miles in four days under close-reefed fore and main topsails. As we were running before the wind we kept ahead of the waves, but every so often one broke right over the ship. It was very fine to watch, and if I had not seen it I would not have believed that waves could rise to such a height. We then picked up the South-East Trades, and crossed the Line again on 12th May.

We anchored at Bombay on 25th May. The coast is very fine, with big mountains covered with palm and coconut trees and the Ghauts in the distance. All our ships had arrived except the Tulloch Castle, but we made a faster passage than any of the ships that left Cove this season. We were able to go ashore for a short time to see a little of the town, and we were all lucky in getting hold of some servants."

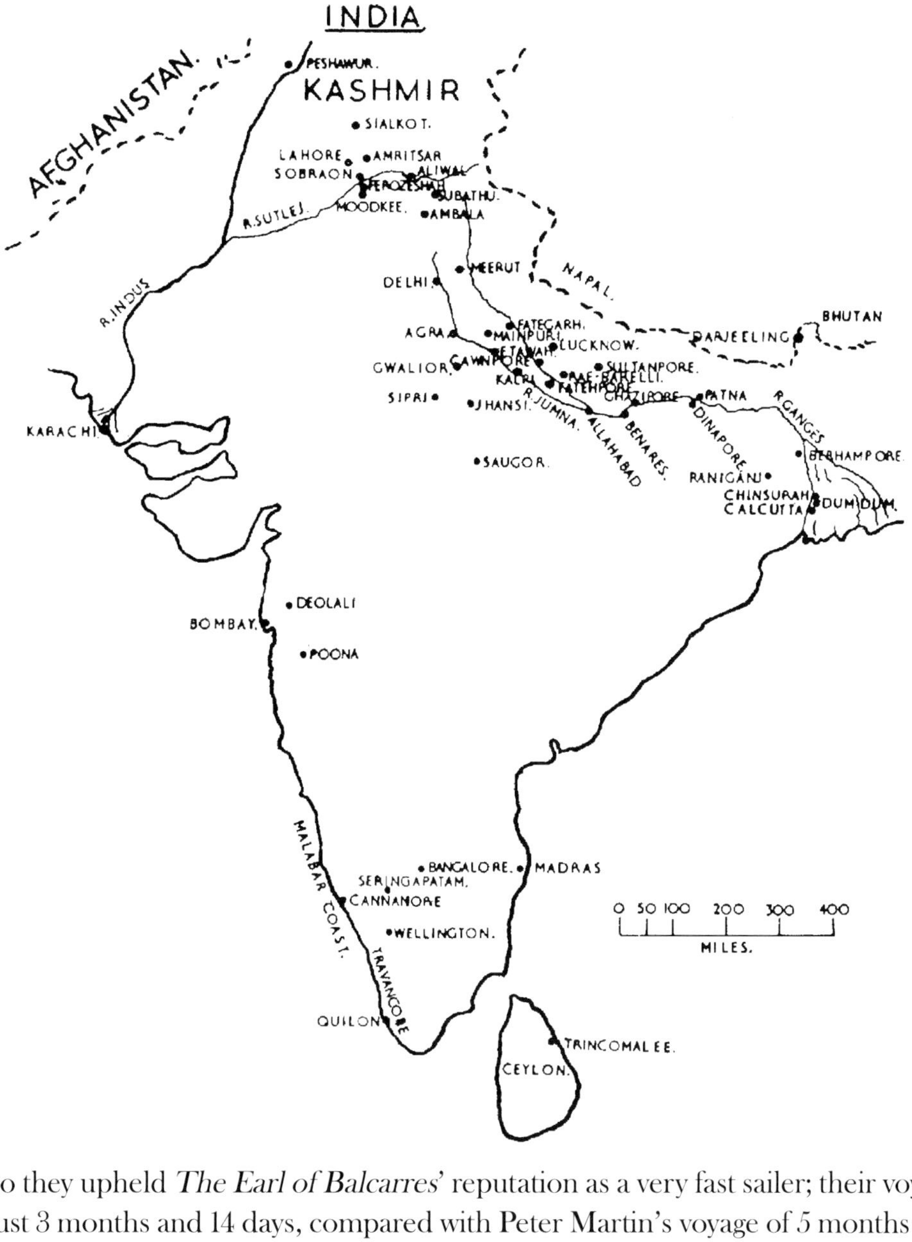

So they upheld *The Earl of Balcarres'* reputation as a very fast sailer; their voyage took just 3 months and 14 days, compared with Peter Martin's voyage of 5 months and 8 days from Portsmouth to Calcutta. *The Tulloch Castle* had started nearly a month before *The Earl of Balcarres*, and reached Bombay a fortnight after her.

In 1758 the 64th Regiment, under Colonel Draper, had been only the second British Regiment to land in India, but that had been in Madras, far to the south. The majority of the troops in India were regiments of the East India Company's army, divided into three Presidencies, but there were always a few British regiments stationed throughout the country, usually for about ten years at a time. The main military centre of the Bombay Presidency was Poona (now known as Pune), which had been ceded to the British after the battle of Koreagon in 1818. It had the advantage of an altitude of 1,000 feet, which gave it a much pleasanter climate for European troops, though it also meant that it could only be reached then, as now, by a very steep road with hair-raising bends.

The military establishment at Poona was a typical army town, laid out with painstaking attention to orderliness and scrupulously cared for, in contrast to the busy and crowded old city, which has been called the spiritual centre of Maharastra, just as Bombay is the commercial centre. This was the destination to which the 64th was heading. It was a trying experience for men in full marching order, who had been confined in cramped quarters with little chance of exercise for more than three months.

7th June 1849 (continued)

"From Bombay we had a two-hour journey in a steamer to Pannivell, and then a march of a mile and a half to a tented camp. After a few hours rest there, we started a march of $12\frac{1}{2}$ miles to the next station, Chooke. This was done at night to avoid the worst of the heat, but it was a very warm night, and from being on board ship so long the men could not march at all, and a great many of them fainted. All the officers hired ponies for the march, but the rascal who said he would bring one for me never did so I had to walk. After the first four miles Lieutenant Grylls was very sick and had to be carried in a palanquin, so I was able to ride his tattoo (that is what they call the ponies) for the rest of the way. We arrived at the encampment at 6 am, just as the sun rose. Our servants had breakfast for us, and I then got an hour's sleep, but by 10am it was so fearfully hot we could not sleep at all. We were surrounded by mountains so that there was scarcely any breeze, and what there was felt as if it had come straight out of an oven, and filled the tents with dust. It was a horrible place. One of the men who was perfectly healthy lay down in the sun for five minutes, and in an hour he was dead. Jeffery was speaking to him at 2 o'clock when he was perfectly well, and at 6 o'clock he buried him.

That night we marched to Khandalla, $13\frac{1}{2}$ miles, and crossed the Ghauts, which was tremendous work. I was lucky enough to meet with a tattoo, or I don't know what I should have done. I went asleep several times on my tattoo, but somehow or other I kept my seat.

We had started at 11 o'clock, and reached the bottom of the mountains at about 2. It is about 6 miles to the top, with some very steep places. The men marched very well, but a great many of them fainted, and lay in the road till they were picked up by the bullock-carts, which were following with the heavy baggage. A few men would not march till we told them that if they remained behind, the hyenas, which we could hear on all sides, would most likely carry them off.

It was quite light before we got to the top, where the scenery was most splendid. The mountains were covered with great trees, and the birds were singing, and the air was so cool and refreshing, that I was quite sorry when the march was over. It had a wonderful effect on the men. A short time before they had been grumbling and were scarcely able to march, and all at once they started singing, so they marched on to Khandalla in fine style.

Near the tents there was a travellers' bungalow, and we all went there. I never saw such a dirty lot as we looked. We had white trousers and our shell jackets open; they were covered in dust, which had also stuck to our hands and faces. We looked as much like tramps as officers. We halted that day at Khandalla, so we all had a good night's rest. The marching had brought on a pain in my side, and the Surgeon of the 83rd, who had come out with us, advised me to go straight on to Poona. I managed to get a seat in a phaeton, and drove straight to Poona. The night after I left the detachment marched through a terrible storm of rain and thunder. It was bad enough in Poona, so it must have been far worse in the mountains. It was a pitch dark night so the lightning was especially vivid. In fact at one time it was such an extraordinary spectacle that every man stopped to watch. The rain was very cool and refreshing, and the officers all say that the men have never marched better than they did on that night, but I am glad I missed it.

When I reported to the Colonel he advised me to take the bungalow which was being built next to his, as it was the only one within a mile of our lines. When the rest came in, Twemlow agreed to share the bungalow with me, for which we pay £5 a month rent."

His friendship with Twemlow must have been helpful to Harry, as well as providing him with congenial company, for Twemlow had been born in India. After going to school in England, he had joined the 4th Foot in India. On its return to England he had transferred into the 64th. His father, a most impressive figure, "6' 3" tall and stout in proportion", had been in India for 37 years, and was a Colonel in the Nizam's service, and also Brigadier of all the troops at Araungabad. His mother had just brought their two daughters, who had been in England since they were three years old, back to India.

"There is a large room in the middle which we use as a sitting room, and a smaller one as a sort of a hall, and on each side a bedroom, and a dressing room and a bathroom. There is nothing in it except matting on the floors, so we have to buy all the furniture, but we shall be able to sell it all when we leave. There are three rows of bungalows, each standing in a large garden, called a compound. They are only one storey high, so the rooms are very lofty. Captain James has got a very good one, with a most beautiful garden.

This is a very large cantonment; besides ourselves there are the 83rd Queen's and the 14th Native Infantry, the 2nd Europeans, a Regiment of Horse Artillery, and some Sappers and Miners, all Company regiments. The 10th Hussars are at Kirkee, about a mile away. Fred Loft is here with the 2nd Europeans."

Frederick James Loft was a distant cousin of Harry's. His father was the Reverend John Loft, who had been Rector of Wyham with Cadeby and Nun Ormesby since 1818. Wyham was even smaller than Healing, with about 25 houses. Nun Ormesby was a 'deserted village' with a handful of houses. At first he was also Vicar of Market Stainton, and lived at Market Stainton House, which he had inherited from his mother. He then moved to Wyham Rectory, and lived there for ten years, before moving to Worthing in Sussex, where he lived until his death in 1884, aged 92, but still Rector of Wyham! Fred was the son of the first of the Reverend John's three wives.

"I feel much better than I have done for a long time, but I still raise a little in the morning. This is one of the most healthy stations in India, with a delightful climate; always cool in the morning and evening all the year round, but now the rainy season is coming it is quite as cool as England, except in the middle of the day.

I have been able to buy rather a nice little horse, so that I shall be able to get out now and see a little of the place. Everyone has one or two horses; in fact riding is the only amusement one has here. (Harry must have been very gratified when James Iles, an old school friend, wrote about the new horse, saying he would sooner take Harry's opinion of a horse than anyone else's. 'You can't have the Loft blood in you, and not know a good horse.')

We all marched to Church at 6 o'clock on Sunday evening. It is a pretty building, about 1½ miles away. The congregation was composed entirely of soldiers and soldiers' wives, because all the English here are in the Army. We have a splendid Mess room, and a Parsee messman who gives us capital dinners. In the hot weather we dine in white suits with a black neckerchief with short collars: it is a very cool and comfortable dress. The Colonel says it is not military, and an order has gone out that we are to wear shell jackets till after the rainy season. On duty we wear shell jackets and white trousers and a white cover over our caps, with part hanging down behind to protect our necks. Altogether it looks very well. We scarcely ever wear our coatees.

I have got two servants and a horse-keeper, pretty good ones I think, but all these natives are great villains and you cannot believe a word they say. My head servant is a fierce looking fellow with a great beard and mustachoes. They all dress in white with red turbans. We are obliged to have a watchman at night. There is a village of regular thieves not far away, and we have to pay one of these rascals. It is absurd and regular blackmail, but if we did not, every thing we have would be stolen. These men will take the sheets off the bed you are sleeping in without waking you.

It is very interesting riding round here, because everything is so different from home. Most of the natives wear very little clothing and the lower castes scarcely any. They drive bullocks instead of horses. They are pretty little things, with a small hump on their shoulders. It takes an awful lot of men to do a simple job, for one man will only do one particular kind of work. The other day James wanted a small bundle of grass carried a few yards, but not one of his servants would do it, as they said they were not hired to carry things. My fellows, luckily for them, do everything I tell them.

I cannot say much for the country. All round there is an immense plain, with no hedges, hardly any trees, and the grass all parched, and with mountains all round in the distance. They say it will change very quickly once the rains come, and the crops and grass will spring up in a few days. We get our pay in rupees. They are as large as half-crowns, and are worth 1/10d. Many things here are very cheap. I paid 2 rupees for some white trousers the other day; jackets are the same, and waistcoats one rupee. A pair of Wellington boots costs two rupees.

We usually get up at about 5.30 am and go out riding until 8.30 when we have a bath and breakfast. We have lunch at about 2 pm and have another ride before dressing for Mess at 6.30 pm. I rode over and called upon Fred Loft the other day. He is looking very well but does not much like India. He told me his father was going to leave Wyham, but I forget where he is going to. Have you heard anything about it? On my way back I also saw something of the city of Poona. It is not nearly so fine as I expected from what I had heard and read of it. All the Palaces and buildings are in ruins, and it is a specimen of decayed grandeur. The Parsees have very nice bungalows and most beautiful gardens. I think India will suit me very well."

Harry started his first letter home on 7th June 1869, and it reached his mother at Louth on 24th August; the first communication she had received from him since he left Cork, six months previously. The posts were not always very reliable, sometimes being disrupted by the monsoon. *"You have no idea of the excitement that is caused here by the report that the mail has reached Bombay."* However Harry did manage to send and receive a monthly letter to and from his mother and his brother. James tried to persuade his mother not to express anxiety in her letters, when there was any sort of delay in receiving correspondence from Harry, in case Harry thought she was blaming him for not having written. Margaret agreed with him in principle, but found it impossible in practice.

The cheaper but slower postal rate was via The Cape and Southampton, which allowed one to send a $\frac{1}{2}$ oz. letter instead of a mere $\frac{1}{4}$ oz. on the faster route by ship to Suez, overland to Port Said, by steamer to Marseilles, and by rail across France. It was not possible to prepay a letter via Marseilles. Using flimsy paper it was possible to send $8\frac{1}{2}$ sheets of thin paper, and by 'crossing' her writing Margaret could send 33 pages of news, gossip, messages from friends, and anxious enquiries about Harry's health. Naturally she was extremely anxious about Harry's physical condition. She must have often remembered how her brother Peter had died in India, just 20 years previously, after only a few months service there, at about the same time as her husband had been dying of consumption, with symptoms only too similar to those Harry had displayed during his illnesses. Nevertheless she apparently remained cheerful and optimistic.

In India Harry's Subdivision was similar to his previous one in Ireland, though the average age was 24, slightly less than previously, because the older men had in most cases not been passed fit for overseas service, and there was a greater proportion of recruits. Harry's old servant, Murphy, was one of the ones to be left behind, to their mutual regret. His Sergeants were R.H. Ecklin, aged 36, from Belfast, with 18 years service, and William Donald, aged 31, a married man from London, who had enlisted 17 years previously at the age of 14, as a Drummer. He was the tallest man in the Subdivision at 5' 10¾".

The Corporals were James Walker, a 21 year-old Dubliner with only 4 years service, and Samuel Wilson, aged 24, from Limerick, with 8 years service. The Corporal's brother, John Wilson, was the Drummer. Of the 56 men, 18 were English, 5 Scottish, and 33 Irish, of whom 22 were Roman Catholics. All the English and Scots were Protestants. Only six of the men were married, one 'without leave'.

The record shows that 2 of the English, 6 of the Irish, and all 5 of the Scots had been court-martialled. The oldest and longest serving private, James McMullin, aged 36 with 18 years service, had the worst record, having been tried by Regimental Court Martial once, and by District Court Martial four times. He cannot have been the easiest of soldiers for a young officer to deal with. Two of the men had been in Harry's previous Subdivision in Ireland. He never mentions any of the NCOs or Privates by name, or in any other way, in his letters home.

Although the 64th wore the Staffordshire Knot as its badge, and had the "Second Staffordshire Regiment" as its full title, there was only one man from Staffordshire in Harry's Subdivision, with a handful from other parts of the Midlands - Coventry, Ashbourne, Nottingham, and Leicester. Captain Pattison, *"a pretty good sort of a fellow, who came to us from the Newfoundland Veterans"*; commanded the Company. For a short time Harry had been in Captain Bingham's Company. He does not give any opinion of the Captain, but remarks, *"Mrs. Bingham is a very fine woman, but she is getting very stout. I think her by far the nicest and best-tempered woman in the Regiment"*.

The 64th had two Lieutenant-Colonels in India. Brevet Lieutenant-Colonel Nicholas Wilson was appointed Second Colonel in August 1848. John Alexander Forbes was Lieutenant-Colonel from 1846 to 1849.

Lists of Officers of the 64th Regiment, showing Harry's rise from junior Ensign to Lieutenant, and the names of colleagues mentioned in his letters.

1847.

64th (The 2nd Staffordshire) Regiment of Foot.

"St. Lucia" - "Surinam".

Colonel.

Sir Richard Bourke, K.C.B.

Lieut. Col.

Severus Wm. Lynam Stretton

Major.

George Duberly

Maximilian James Western

Captain.

James Draper

William John James

Charles Norris

Fred. Arth. Errington

Ambrose Barcroft Parker

Harry Altham Cumberlege

Ramsay Hankey Smith

Westcote Whitchurch Lyttleton

Hon. Geo. Fred: Wm. Yelverton

William Baillie Jopp

Lieutenant.

John Canavan

Francis Henry Kilvington

Thomas Stirling

Willoughby Harcourt Carter

Charles Scott Jeffery

George William Powlett

Hon. James Lyon Bingham Browne

Isaac Temple Twinning

William Stephens

continued:-

John Buchanan Burne

Wm. Helsham Candler

Neville Hill Shute

Robt. Bickerstaff

Ensign.

Robert Mockler

Alfred Picton Bowlby

Joseph Singleton

Robert du Cane

John Henry Capel Loft

Charles Thompson

Hen. Rob. Crew Godley

Edw. William Armstrong

Paymaster.

John Ralston

Adjutant.

Willoughby Harcourt Carter

Qua:-Master.

James Howe

Surgeon.

William Smith

Assist. Surg:

William Purdon M.D.

Facings black.

Agent, Messrs. Cox & Co.

1848-49.

64th (The 2nd Staffordshire) Regiment of Foot.

St. Lucia - Surinam.

Colonel.

Sir Rich. Bourke K.C.B.

Lieut. Col.

Severus Wm. Lynam Stretton

Major.

George Duberley
Maximilian James Western

Captain.

James Draper
William John James
Charles Norris
Fred. Arth. Errington
Ambrose Barcroft Parker
Harry Altham Cumberlege
Hon. George Frederick William Yelverton
John Canavan
Francis Henry Kilvington
Charles Pattison

Lieutenant.

Thomas Stirling
Willoughby Harcourt Carter
Charles Scott Jeffery
George William Powlett Bingham
Hon. James Lyon Browne
Isaac Temple Twinning
John Buchanan Burne
Wm. Helsham Candler
Neville Hill Shute
Robert Mockler
Henry Francis

continued:-

Alfred Picton Bowlby
Josiah Marshall Heath

Ensign.

Robert du Cane
John Henry Capel Loft
Charles Thompson
Hen. Rob. Crew Godley
Edw. William Armstrong
William John Chads
William Bell
William Davies Shipley

Paymaster.

James Homes

Adjutant.

Willoughby Harcourt Carter

Qua:- Master.

John Sears

Surgeon.

William Smith

Asst: Surg:

William Purdon M.D.

Facings black.

Agent, Messrs. Cox & Co.

1849-50.

64th (The 2nd Staffordshire) Regiment of Foot.

"St Lucia" – "Surinam".

continued: –

Colonel.

Sir Rich. Bourke K.C.B.

Lieut. Col.

James Stopford

Nicholas Wilson K.H.

Major.

Maximilian Jas. Western

James Draper

Captain.

William John James

Fred. Arthur Errington

Harry Altham Cumberlege

Charles Pattison

Thomas Stirling

Charles Scott Jeffery

Geo. Wm. Powlett Bingham

Frederick Holland

Charles William Sibley

Charles Stewart Cochrane

Lieutenant.

Isaac Temple Twinning

John Buchanan Burne

Wm. Helsham Candler

Neville Hill Shute

Robert Mockler

Henry Francis

Alfred Picton Bowlby

Robert du Cane

Charles Thompson

William John Chads

Sydney Cotton

Wm. Fletcher James Morphy

Richard Charles Mc Crea

Mathew Fanning

Geo. Hamilton Twemlow

Arthur Edward Molloy

Arch. Edward Cochrane Forster

Doveton Downes Greentree

Chas. Fred. Brockman

Godfrey Lyon Knight

Walter Johnston

John Henry Capel Loft

William Bell

Ensign.

William Davies Shipley

Horatio Glynn Grylls

John Austin Moultrie

Augustus Applewhaite

Francis Fothergill Hood

Hen. Hammerton Alexander

Fred. T. Hutchison

Standish de Courcy O'Grady

Paymaster.

James Howes

Adjutant.

John B. Burne

Qua.-Master.

John Sears

Surgeon.

George Archer M.D.

Assist. Surgeon.

Henry Crisp, M.B.

Wm. Henry Short

And. Leith Adams, M.D

Facings black.

1850-51.

64th (The 2nd Staffordshire) Regiment of Foot.

"St Lucia" - "Surinam".

Colonel.

Sir Richard Bourke K.C.B.

Lieut. Col.

James Stopford C.B.
Nicholas Wilson K.H.

Major.

Maximilian James Western
James Draper

Captain.

William John James
Harry Altham Cumberlege
Charles Pattison
Thomas Stirling
Charles Scott Jeffery
George Wm. Powlett Bingham
Frederick Holland
Charles William Sibley
Charles Stuart Cochrane
Isaac Temple Twinning

Lieutenant.

Wm. Helsham Candler
Neville Hill Shute
Robert Moekler
Henry Francis
Alfred Picton Bowlby
Robert du Cane
Charles Thompson
William John Chads
Sydney Cotton
Wm. Fletcher James Morph
Richard Cha. M'Crea
Matthew Fanning
Geo. Hamilton Twenlow

continued:-

Arthur Edward Mulloy
Arch. Edw. Cochrane Forster
Doveton Downes Greentree
Chas. Frederick Brockman
Godfrey Lyon Knight
John Henry Capel Loft
William Bell
William Davies Shipley
Horatio Glynn Grylls
John Austin Moultrie

Ensign.

Augustus Applewhaite
Francis Fothergill Hood
Hen. Hammerton Alexander
Fred. T. Hutchison
Standish de Courcy O'Grady
Valentine Ryan
David Mortimer Murray
Alfred John Tuke

Paymaster.

James Homes

Adjutant.

William Bell

Qua.-Master.

John Sears

Surgeon.

George Archer, M.D.

Assist. Surgeon.

Henry Crisp M.B.
Wm. Henry Short
Edward John Kennedy M.D.

The battle of Reshire in Persia, at the moment when Colonel Stopford was killed at the head of the 64th Regiment.

The siege of Lucknow in 1857.
The 64th Regiment were involved in the attempts to relieve the garrison.

The battle of Sobraon 1844 (Sikh War) in Northern India had involved the 80th Regiment of Foot (Staffordshire Volunteers). This illustration shows the ferocity of battle.

The Colours of the 64th Regiment, presented to them at Weedon in 1844, and often carried by Harry. The picture shows them in the tattered state after the Indian Mutiny.

The 64th Regiment landing from a steamer in Persia at the start of the campaign there.

CHAPTER 9
LIFE IN POONA

Harry seems to have settled down to life in cantonments fairly quickly, though occasionally he spoke of being a little unsettled. It is hard to tell exactly what his relations were with his brother officers. In his letters he mentions them only briefly, either saying of one of them that he was a nice fellow, or to speak disparagingly of their horsemanship.

17th July 1849

"We have been having very fine weather and the climate continues to suit me very well. My usual dress in the house is a shirt and a pair of 'pyjamas' - very thin loose trousers which tie round the waist - and when I am out of doors I wear white trousers and a jacket and a wickerwork hunting cap with a white cover.

I was very much disgusted at being sent to drill soon after we arrived here. Every sub. junior to the Adjutant was hard at work at the goose-step for 2 hours every morning and afternoon. Burne was in his glory and marched us about in great style. This delightful work lasted for ten days, when the Colonel inspected us, declared that we performed to admiration, and dismissed us forthwith. For some time we had nothing to do but orderly duty, but now we parade at 6 o'clock every day except Saturday. For two days last week General Manson, a Company's officer, who spoke very highly of the Regiment in his report, inspected us. The old fellow and his staff dined with us on Saturday, when 43 sat down to dinner. The Colonel is a smart officer and a very nice person, but a very hot fiery fellow, and swears like a trooper, with two or three medals and clasps.

There were two grand balls given here last week, one by the officers of the staff, and one by Lord Faulkland, but I did not go to either. I never did much care for that sort of thing, and here the ladies are all either old married women, or else girls looking for a husband. Some of our fellows talk of entering their horses for the next races, but they have little idea about riding, and no idea of how to train a horse. A lot of the fellows have arabs, but I could not afford one. Mine is a very strong, short-legged little dark chestnut country-bred. He is only 4 years old, so he will improve. He carries me capitally and can walk and gallop with most of them. He does much more work than most of them, as they are afraid of using their horses, and keep tattoos to save them. I use mine on all occasions and he is always ready to go. He jumps well too, and I had him over every fence near the lines before I had had him a week.

I have a pretty good country greyhound and Twemlow has another so, as hares are very plentiful, we have great sport coursing. They are not as fast as English dogs, but the hares are little ones and not as fast as English ones. We had great fun the other day hunting a jackal. We assembled a pack of terriers and curs of all descriptions, and after a short run ran into him in great style, but none of the dogs would face him, so he was picked up and turned out again with a good start. He gave us another pretty run before he went to ground - or rather water!

In the cantonments there are a great number of half-wild dogs, which they call pariahs. Some of the fellows hunt them with spears, but I would not want to kill the poor brutes. There is a plentiful supply of pigeons, and we have pigeon-shooting now and then. I can sometimes knock them over pretty well. They are wild blue pigeons, and at 21 yards with a trap that shoots them up into the air, you have to shoot very quickly and very straight or they are off to the mountains like demons. There is a club called 'The Jim Khana' got up by the regiments for cricket and pigeon-shooting etc., but I do not belong to it, as I do not think cricket would be very good for me yet.

I do not have much to do with the natives. Some of the men are tall but very slight, and some are fine-looking fellows, but the women are frightful. Some are very dark, and some are sort of yellow. The Parsees are very nearly as fair as we are. They are fire-worshippers and came originally from Persia. They are very respectable and mostly very rich. They wear slippers turned up at the toes, red or yellow pyjamas, a white garment between a shirt and a coat, and a cap without any sort of peak, exactly like a flower. The lower classes wear a turban and a piece of cloth rolled round their loins".

20th July (continued)

"We had some capital fun yesterday when some of the fellows got up two steeple-races over all the compounds. It was one of the funniest sights you could imagine."

Harry then goes on to give a full account of the races with as much detail about the course, the horses and the riders, as if he were describing a major Lincolnshire steeplechase. *"There were several heats over 12 fences and 2 hurdles."* Harry's friend, Shute, won in a workmanlike style, and Greentree provided a lot of the amusement. *"A very conceited fellow, who came to us from the Ceylon Rifles, and thinks himself a tearing rider. He came out in top boots and spurs, with a black waistcoat and a hunting cap, but at the second fence went clean over his horse's head. He remounted but then his horse bolted and nearly carried him into a bungalow; he was last seen clinging on to the pony's neck, with one spur caught in his stirrup.*

Twemlow and I went out shooting very early this morning. We went several miles out into the country, but as it was the first time we had been out, we did not know the best places to find any game. We did see a few antelopes but we could not get near them, because they were in open country and we were wearing white clothes.

We had the 1st Grenadiers N.I. to dinner last night, which was not a large party as there are very few officers in the Native regiments. We are to feast all the regiments in Poona, as they have all been very civil to us. When the 83rd and the 10th dine with us we shall have a tremendous party. Can you please find out for certain whether a player in a game of chess can have two Queens on the board at the same time? There is a great dispute among the fellows on this point."

This letter, which Harry had started on 17th July, did not reach Margaret until 4th October.

20th August 1849

"I have quite given up hope for your letter which I should have received when we landed in Bombay. It must have been lost, which is most annoying, for you know how much I reckon hearing of your proceedings. We were lucky to have a good new bungalow, as in the wet weather, which I hope is now over, two oldish ones and several stables fell down.

A very melancholy thing happened yesterday evening. Errington, one of our Captains, fell down dead. It was awfully sudden. He commanded the Church Parade, and appeared in perfect health. He marched the men off, but after he had gone a short way he turned back, saying he did not feel very well. As he was walking home he fell down, and by the time anybody could reach him he was dead. It has not yet been ascertained whether he died from apoplexy or a stroke of the sun. He was a very nice fellow, and much liked by everyone.

The races are going on now, and the people of Poona are making desperate attempts at being gay, as anything like amusement is rarely to be met with here, and when there is any, people try to make it last as long as possible. So there are only two race days in each week, but they make them last for three weeks. The races are at Kirkee, about four miles from this. I have been twice and enjoyed myself very much. Most of the people here have been out for some time, so it is very interesting to see the different turn-outs. I saw several hats and coats which might have come out of the Ark.

I had a slight accident when I was there on Friday, which might have been serious. I was watching a race on my horse when a chigrand (a vehicle very like a cab) ran against us and nearly knocked us both over. Someone had left it unattended, and the shouting, when the horses were passing, frightened it and it ran away. It came at me from behind, so I neither saw nor heard anything until part of it hit my leg. The step caught my horse in the body and made a nasty cut. I lost my hat and a girth and a stirrup leather but was very little hurt. I rode home quietly, and he is not much the worse off for our adventure, but I shall not be able to put a saddle on him for a week or more.

There have been several balls lately, but I have not been to any of them, as there are always very few ladies, and it is extremely hard to get a partner. The 10th Horse gave a very grand Ball last week - those worthies do dance in this country. The first year they were here they gave a ball, but as they had never called upon anyone, not one lady would go to it. This did them a great deal of good, and since then they have been very civil."

(Some years previously the officers of the 10th had been the source of much amusement and derision when they had declared, in answer to an invitation, "the Tenth do not dance".)

"Mrs. James asks to be remembered to you, and to say that your letter to her did not reach Cork until after we had sailed, so it was much delayed, but she will answer it shortly. The children are both very well. She likes this country very much. At home she was not very much thought about, but here she has her carriage, and, as ladies are scarce, she is made a great deal of, and has no end of partners at all the balls. She is in her element here, and is very conceited already. I was only in Bingham's Company for a short time. When we got here we were all changed around, and I am now with Pattison, a pretty good sort of fellow, an old bachelor who came to us from the Newfoundland Veterans. Mrs. Bingham is a very fine woman, but is getting rather stout. I think her the nicest and best-tempered woman in the Regiment.

I have just been obliged to send away two of my servants. My head boy (they are all called boys out here - when I want something I always call out 'Boy!') because I could not get him to do anything, and the horse-keeper for stealing some money from one of Twemlow's servants. I have got two more, but they are all rascals. I defy anyone to keep his temper with them. We have been having two dinner parties a week for the last month, but they are all over now, thank goodness, so we can have a bit of quiet. The Parsee mess man gives us capital dinners, just like we had at home. We get our wine from France, salmon, ale and porter from England, and everything else comes from this country. I am not much taken with the Indian fruits, except for the grapes, which are very fine, though they look very well as dessert. We have mangos, pineapples, plantains, custard apples, pomegranates, sweet limes, shaddocks, melons, oranges, etc. I dare say all very good if you care for that sort of thing, but I would much sooner have a good English apple or plum. Some of these, together with gooseberries and rhubarb are brought out here, but the voyage does not do them much good. The greatest luxury we have is ice. Everything we drink is iced. There is always a lump of it in our tumblers or wine glasses."

(By 1845 ice cut from the lake at Wenham, Massachusetts, was being taken to India, with a double crossing of the equator, and brought a good profit to the shippers.)

Many of our officers are trying for exchange because they are disgusted with this country, but I like it and the climate, because I can keep a horse and do many of the things which I could not do at home. I am very well and strong, but have not been able to get weighed. I have got a good deal of colour, both red and brown! I have no unpleasant feelings in my chest, but I raise a little when I first get up in the morning. The boil is all right now, and has not troubled me since I left home. I have an excellent appetite. I have not grown at all; I fancy I have given that up all together by now. I look after myself very well. There, dear Mother, that answers all your questions!

Who do you think is our Interpreter at present? Tommy Anderson! He came down from Belgaum about a month since, but I never thought of his being the person in the picture which I have often admired. About three days ago some one told me that Anderson had said that he knew something about me, and then it struck me who he was. He is a nice-looking little fellow, with dark hair, blue eyes, and beautiful small features. We see very little of him as he lives in the 14th's lines, and he does no regimental duty".

Tommy Anderson and Harry had been "two little boys together in Carlow", as Margaret reminded Harry. Tommy's father had been the Surgeon of the 92nd while Thomas Capel Loft was serving in it, and had maintained his friendship with Margaret, and with her sister, Christina, over the intervening years by correspondence, but they had only met once when Margaret and her sons visited Edinburgh.

"Two of our officers are studying hard at Hindustani, and will be examined at Bombay in October. If one of them passes, Anderson will have to give up the Interpretership, as it is always given to an officer of the Regiment if there is one qualified for it. Twemlow is one of them, and he has the great advantage of having lived in the country for many years. When I have got a little money I shall have a try at it. You need two munshees (natives who teach the language) and they cost 45 rupees a month.

We shall all have to buy tents soon. The Colonel has to send in a certified statement that every officer has a serviceable tent and is in every respect ready for active service. One of our Ensigns, Hood, is a very nice fellow, who comes from Lincolnshire. He tells me Askew Floyer is to be a married to some rather grand person. Hood is some relation of Mrs. Danby, but he does not admire old Danby at all.

Today is the hottest day I have ever know, but people who have been in the country before seem to feel it more than the rest of us do. Sometimes Twemlow, who was born here, complains of the heat, when I think it quite pleasant."

Harry started this letter on 29th August, and sent it by Marseilles, so that it reached Margaret on the same day as his previous letter, which had travelled round the Cape.

12th September 1849

"We have had a spell of wet weather again, as the monsoon is breaking up. I have had a little cold so put myself on the sick list for a few days. Everything goes on as usual here, but we have been getting up a little diversion among ourselves lately. Our races came off on Monday and Tuesday, and were very good indeed. Everyone

thought them much better than the ones at Kirkee. The Ladies behaved very handsomely and made up a Purse, worth 150 rupees. Mrs. Stopford, the Colonel's wife, has given a beautiful gold-mounted whip to be run for. There are a great many horses entered for it. There was a most amusing race for the Cheroot Stakes, where every jockey has to smoke a cigar throughout the race, and if the first rider at the finish has not got his cigar burning, he loses. Alexander won it on a horse of Thompson's. Far more horses were entered for the races here, and they were pretty equally matched, while at Kirkee there were one or two really good horses who had nothing to run against.

I entered my horse for a hurdle race. The horses were all given special names for the race card, and Shute put my horse down as 'The Uncle' (it seems likely that Harry's fellow-officers had heard a great deal about *'My Uncle who won the Liverpool), but although I was fit enough myself, the horse was not fully recovered from its injury at Kirkee, and I had to pull it up after* $\frac{3}{4}$ *of a mile, to my great disappointment. He was clearing the hurdles better than any of them, but he had not regained his stamina, and as I was two stone heavier than the other riders, it was too much to expect of him.*

Twemlow's horse, 'The Rocket', won the Galloway Race easily, ridden by little Alexander. He only weights 7st. 2lb. so if he is on anything that can go at all, he is almost sure to win. Another of Twemlow's horses won the Ladies Prize, and 'The Rocket' won the Handicap for Mrs. Stopford's whip for Twemlow, so he did very well. Poor Shute was going to the post in that race, when his horse bolted and never stopped for $1\frac{1}{2}$ *miles. Some of the riders were in racing costume, but I wore white trousers and a white silk coat, which I had borrowed.*

We have got up a Theatre in the Regiment, at which the Privates are the actors. It opened last night, and the performance was excellent. Some of the Captains have taken a great deal of trouble over it, getting the dresses and taking the rehearsals. The men acted wonderfully well. It will be a good thing for the men. The poor fellows have nothing in the world to amuse them here, and are much worse off than the officers.

I think there will be a few steps going before long. Burne has sent in his papers; he has never been well since he came to India. It would never do for him to exchange, as he is at the top of the Lieutenants' list, so he is going to leave the Army. He has put in for the Adjutancy of the North Lincolnshire Militia, as Captain Kennedy is retiring. Bell is to succeed Burne as Adjutant. He gave Burne £100 to induce him to give it up, and also to use his influence with the Colonel to get it for him. Bell is a nice gentlemanly little fellow, and in time will make a good Adjutant. He is below me so he cannot drill me, which is a great comfort.

There is a report that we are to go to Belgaum. I should be happy to go there as it is by far the best quarter in India. It is a very healthy place, and in the cold weather they have to have fires. One wing of the 78th is going to Bombay, and the other to Aden, which is a miserable place and fearfully hot. You cannot venture outside the walls without running the risk of being shot by the Arabs. Anderson hopes that neither of our fellows will pass at the examination next month so that he can remain with us. He is a nice gentlemanly person and a good officer. He likes India very much.

We have got a new Colonel now called Wilson. He exchanged with Duberly after we left Ireland, and only arrived here the other day. Anderson says his father knows him well, because he was in the 92nd a long time ago. I hear he is a nice fellow, but a great Tartar; a hot fiery man, who swears like a trooper. He has 3 or 4 medals and clasps. At the Kirkee races I saw the Abymers of Terode who commanded the troops fighting against Sir C. Napier in the late wars in Scinde. They were taken prisoner and live in a large bungalow here. They are fine looking men with huge beards, and ride about with their great swords, followed by two of their irregular cavalry as a sort of guard of honour, but are not allowed to leave the cantonments.

My cold is much better, but because of the bad weather I shall remain on the sick list for another day or two. Our races are still going on, but I have not been out for the last two days. There was a donkey race yesterday, which was an absurd affair and caused a lot of fun.

Sir Willoughby Cotton, the Commander in Chief of the Presidency, has inspected the regiment. He was delighted with us, and thinks in a short time it will be the finest and best disciplined Regt. in India. The men went through their movements, but not so well as they did in Ireland, which is to be expected since they have scarcely ever been drilled out here, and have not yet got accustomed to the Colonel's word of command. The old General dined with us last week; he is immensely stout, and is not blessed with a very good temper, but he is very clever and straightforward, and is altogether well liked. I believe Sir Charles Napier is going home, and Sir Willoughby is to be made Commander in Chief of India. The old General is immensely stout.

I was not surprised to hear of the poor old General's death. I think it is a happy release. What has become of the poor unfortunate boy? I was sorry to hear about Uncle Charles. What a miserable life he must have endured these last few years! I wonder what he will do. It will be a capital thing for the children. I cannot imagine what would have happened to them if they had remained in Grimsby."

This letter was posted at Poona on 12th September and received by Margaret at Louth on 6th November.

Margaret's long letters were always full of family news. She had told Harry of the death of his grandfather, John Henry Loft, at the age of 80. During a long, often controversial, life he had attained the rank of Lieutenant General, and had represented Grimsby in the House of Commons, but his later years were spent in obscurity, after marital and financial difficulties. It is ironical that he died in poverty, in the street in Grimsby, which had been named Loft Street in his honour many years before, to show the town's appreciation of the contribution he had made to its growing prosperity. The identity of 'The unfortunate boy' is a mystery. From other sources it seems possible that he was an illegitimate son of the old man. It is certain that he did not have Loft as his surname, and that he was for a time an inmate of the Union workhouse at Louth. The fact that the page in the book containing the names of all the people admitted to the Union at that time has been torn out, only adds to the mystery.

The fine west door of Healing Church.
The author and his younger son - great grandson and great great grandson of Thomas Loft.

Of the General's sons, John, William, Henry and Fred attended his funeral at Marshchapel. They were the only mourners. Ingram had gone to Australia and disappeared. James, Gilbert, and Thomas had died. Charles was unable to be present, because he was playing cricket for the 22 Gentlemen of Hull against the All England eleven.

Charles was the 'Uncle Charles' referred to in Harry's letter. He too had his share of matrimonial and financial troubles, which had recently come to a crisis. He had lost his position in a wine-merchant's firm, incurred large debts and parted from his wife. His children were lodged in a cottage at Healing, where they were the objects of the villagers' pity, while their uncle, Fred, was living in style at Healing House. Charles later became Station Master of the railway station at Stallingborough, the next village to Healing. He was probably the first, and possibly the only, Old Etonian Station Master.

14th October 1849

"That letter which I should have received from you when we arrived in India has now been found! Bowlby stayed in Bombay after Headquarters left, and the Agent gave him your letter which had arrived the very day before we landed. When he got up here the coat he was wearing was put away and he forgot all about it, till the other

day when he was again going to Bombay and put the same coat on, and of course found the letter in the pocket. I was very annoyed, thinking how much I should have enjoyed reading it as soon as I had landed, but I did not say too much to Bowlby, because I know how easy it is to make a mistake.

I have been on the sick list for the last month with an ulcerated sore throat. I have been rubbing it with croton oil, and it is rather painful whenever I move. It is the most horrible sore throat I have ever had, and very painful, but I think it is getting better now. I go out riding every day, but I do no duty and dine at home. I was surprised that you did not hear sooner of my arrival in Bombay as I saw in an English paper an account of the arrival of the Earl of Balcarres, and my name was mentioned in it.

I told you that Burne has sent in his papers. Well, Sir Charles Napier thought it very strange for him to sell, when he is at the top of the list, and refused to accept his papers, so they have been sent to the Horse Guards, and poor Burne has to return from Bombay and remain here till he receives an answer from home. Johnston, the great 6ft. 4in. man has also sent in his papers. He has been on the sick list ever since he came out. He pretended to be very ill, but he was drinking hard the whole time. However he humbugged the Doctor and got a month's sick leave in Bombay. About a week after he left here we heard that he was in Bombay Hospital as mad as a March hare with delirium tremens. The Colonel has ordered him to send in his papers at once. He is a wild quarrelsome Irishman, and is no loss to the Regiment. He used to be drunk early in the day, but his medical advisers thought it was just his little peculiarity. I shall get two steps.

I regret to say that we have had cholera among the men, and have lost a great number. The first six men to get it died in about four hours. The others naturally got frightened and started drinking, which was the worst thing they could do. The Sergeant Major, a very steady man indeed, drank steadily for some time; he had cholera but got over it, and then died a few days later of delirium tremens. Only one officer, Shipley the Junior Ensign, had it. He was desperately ill for twelve hours, but is now over the worst.

Dr. Archer has married a young girl to whom his son once paid a great deal of attention. Archer was not married at home, as he was obliged to come out in a troopship, and it would have been uncomfortable for both of them. It is bad enough being by yourself in a small cabin, but with a wife as well it must be something dreadful. So she came over land, and they were married in Bombay.

I have not yet seen Colonel Wilson. He was on leave at Bombay for a long time, and since I have been on the sick list I have not been able to call upon him. Twemlow has gone up to Aurangabad to see his father, so I have the bungalow to myself at present. I am glad that Uncle Fred is now comfortably settled at Healing. It is bad luck for him and Uncle William having to pay £500 for Uncle Charles.

Who can have put all that curious stuff in the paper about the poor old General; they certainly made no effort to stick to the truth. I am glad the poor boy has been taken care of. (The Lincolnshire papers had carried an obituary of the General in which scarcely one fact was true. Margaret had told Harry that the poor boy's Aunt had felt so dull without him that she had taken him out of the Union.) *I think the Queen was quite right to go to Ireland. They are an excitable set of rascals, and her visit will probably do good, and help to settle them."*

I shall think of you all at Christmas. I wish I were spending it with you, but I hope we shall spend many, many ones together yet. I sometimes think of us all being together some time in the future at Healing, if your plans for Jem work out."

It was going to be Uncle Fred's turn, as one of the two landowners in Healing, to appoint a new Rector for the parish, whenever a vacancy should occur. Margaret had made up her mind that Jem was to be ordained, so that Fred could appoint him to the Rectory. She was busy making enquiries about the cost of various universities and the chance of getting financial help from every possible source, and some unlikely ones. One plan was for Jem to go to Trinity College, Dublin, and for Margaret to move to that city.

"I saw in a paper that the Twenty Two of Hull cut a very poor figure against the All England men. I suppose the bowling was too good for them. Now that Uncle Fred is comfortably settled I suppose Healing is more like its old self. You must tell me about all the changes. I am very glad that old Crisp is back with Uncle again; he is a worthy fellow."

Uncle Fred and Gloriana, his new bride, had taken up residence at Healing House. The house had been neglected for a long time, and extensive repairs were necessary before it was a suitable home for the newly-weds. Uncle John had been asked to supervise the repairs, but since he was considered dilatory even in a family which was noted for its dilatory ways, it took much longer than Fred liked. Crisp had been persuaded to return, and although he was officially the groom, he became a sort of major-domo in the household. Together with all the other servants he was now wearing livery.

"A short time since all the horses were led about the lines covered in flowers and preceded by a band of native musicians, making a most horrible row. Afterwards the horses are all assembled, and goats are sacrificed and prayers offered up for them. Neither Twemlow nor I would let our horses go. His horse-keeper was very much annoyed, but mine, being a Madrassi man, did not care a straw. You cannot walk 100 yards without seeing huge idols; they are hideous looking things and generally painted red."

This letter was posted on 15th October and reached Louth on 27th November, having travelled by the overland route.

In all Harry's letters there is no mention in his letters of any form of military training apart from drilling; musketry is never referred to, neither are Field Days. In fact his life, on the evidence of the letters, could have been that of a young gentleman of leisure. Yet he was serving in a regiment which was shortly to see active service. Moreover it was part of an army which in a few years was to fight the Russians in the Crimea, and to be involved in the ghastly events of the Mutiny.

In addition to his family letters, Harry heard from, and wrote to, many of his friends at Louth, who were leading very different lives from his. Among them was John Hodgson Iles, whose father had a very large farm at Binbrook Hill. He had gone from Louth Grammar School to Lincoln College, Oxford. His letter gives a vivid, but not very attractive, impression of mid-nineteenth century undergraduate life, although perhaps some allowance should be made for a desire to impress a distant friend.

"Term is just over, and so before I leave for the Long Vacation I may as well give you a little information as to what has been happening to me since your departure. Of course up here it is the old routine of life, varied by this part of the year being the great boating time. I pulled in the eight oar, and Lincoln finished 7th out of 20 boats, having got up three places this year so we made up a very fair boat, and put on at Maidenhead Regatta. The course was about 2 miles with the stream, but on the day of the race there was a strong head wind, which added about another mile of work. However we had not a very hard race and won, whereby each of the crew has a silver medal, and we hold for a year a Grand Challenge Cup, value 100 guineas, which you may imagine is pretty often filled with champagne on grand occasions. I also pulled in the pair oar races, but lost.

In the evening of the Regatta, as winning crew we gave a champagne supper to about 50 men, which ended at three o'clock with most of the men pretty far gone. Everyone then went out into the town, and I never saw bells and knockers and sign posts come down so quick. No one dare oppose us, though the cads had assembled in large numbers before we parted. Not being so far gone as some I assisted in getting some to bed, particularly one of our crew, who fought like a young Chinaman, till he catted so bad that he was obliged to submit. People looked very savage next day, but we left the place before they could muster any evidence, or proceed to extremes.

I am going to spend the Long Vacation in North Wales with a reading party, and go in for my final examination next November, after which I shall have very nearly done with Oxford, a circumstance I rather regret, as on the whole we have a splendid time of it up here. Next year I shall have nothing to do but go about larking, till I begin reading Divinity for Ordination; then the sooner I get a fat living the better.

I have not been home since Christmas, but I hear rumours about the bad times for farmers down there; in fact there are meetings all over the country to consider some remedy for the present agricultural distress, but nothing seems to be done. I think it is a bad trade just now, and James (his cousin) *will have to look smartish when he takes one for himself, and take to smoking shag tobacco instead of cigars, with some muddy swipes to wet his whistle."*

Shortly afterwards Hodgson continued the tale:

"I am now lodging with six other men in a very pleasant little village in Merionethshire, surrounded by the most splendid scenery. The last week has been so hot we have done nothing but eat, drink, smoke and bathe, but when it is cooler we shall take some excursions, and go up Snowdon and other mountains. We should think we had run quite out of the world, if it were not for some coaches passing through daily. Many of the people cannot speak a single word of English, and the women go about with bare feet and large hats, with very broad brims, and tapering upwards like a sugar loaf.

Snowdon c1850
Snowdon and Oxford must have seemed a long way away for Harry.

We enjoy our mode of life immensely, doing a very fair amount of reading, with a little whist, etc. Two of the party are obliged to live immensely temperately, being troubled with the 'Venereal'. We stayed a night at Chester on our way; the women there are a very pretty race, the town old and curious. But at Bangor the difficulty is to find an ugly girl. They are most tremendous stunners. The only English most of them know consisted of their being able to call us 'scamps'.

The curate of this village has just called, and offered us the use of his library, cricket things, and some pews in church, so after all this civility we shall be obliged to go to church very often. The only other respectable inhabitant in the place is an old lady, who owns most of the property, so with no notion of being respectable, or wishing to be, we can go about in any dress, smoking long clays, which is rather a sweet liberty after the restrictions of Oxford."

Hodgson Iles was ordained in due course, and eventually became the highly respected Archdeacon of Wolverhampton.

CHAPTER 10

HARRY'S LAST VOYAGE

Harry was obviously enjoying life in India, though in his letters he often expressed his regrets that he would not see his mother and brother again for many years, and he always wanted to know what they had been doing, and what was happening at Healing. He appears to have avidly read and re-read the long letters he received each month. His mother must have been disturbed when he started to mention some problems with his health, after only four months in India. First he developed 'a cold', which he thought had been brought on by getting wet in the monsoon. It did not clear up, and he developed a terribly ulcerated throat as we have seen. He wrote to his mother to say *"I am on the sick list for a few days"*, having assured her only a month before *"I am well and strong now, and my appetite is very good indeed".*

12th November 1849

"I have not been able to get rid of my sore throat, which has been annoying me very much. Sometimes they could scarcely hear me speak, and when I swallowed anything the pain was most horrible. I was practically choking and coughing violently. I had my throat leeched, and rubbed with croton oil. I tried all sorts of gargle, but nothing did me any good

At last they put on a Belladonna plaister, which has entirely taken away the pain, but I am still very hoarse. My cough too is better, but it still bothers me in a morning when I raise a great deal of light coloured stuff every morning. I have lost flesh lately, but that is because I have not been able to take much exercise. I sometimes have a ride but walking is difficult. The boil is just as usual; it has not discharged since I left home. I hope I shall be able to give you a better account before long.

Archer, (the Regimental Surgeon) *thinks change of air will do me good, and has recommended that I go to Bombay, so I have applied for two months leave, and expect to start tomorrow or the next day. I have sent my horse and my baggage on, as they will be four days on the road. I shall take a phaeton, and post down. The vehicles they call phaetons are large double-seated carriages with tops to them, and are very comfortable. I have written to the Agent to take me a house, so that when I get there my things will have arrived, and everything will be ready for me. I shall be in the care of the Inspector General of Hospitals, a very clever man. I hope that he, together with the sea breezes, will soon set me to rights.*

We received orders last week to hold ourselves in readiness for Scinde, and expect to move to Karrachee about the end of this month. The Regiment will march down to Pannivel and then go in steamers to Karrachee. The married people are in a terrible state, as they were certain we should remain here for a couple of years, and

Harry Loft painted by Zephanaiah Bell, a month
before he sailed for India.

have bought no end of things, which they will have to take with them at very great expense, or sell them for a mere nothing at all. I have been busy selling my furniture, and have got one of the fellows to take my half of the bungalow."

16th November

"Here I am in Bombay, dear Mother. I left Poona at 6 o'clock on Wednesday night. I had the phaeton closed up, and contrived to sleep most of the way, tho' it shook horribly. I arrived at Khandala at 12, and got into a palanquin and was carried down the Ghaut. I got into another phaeton, which got me to Pannivel by 7 o'clock. I had breakfast there, and at 12 sailed for Bombay in a Bunder boat, a small boat with two masts and a raised cabin at the stern. There was very little wind, and the men had to row most of the way. I made myself as comfortable as I could in the little cabin, but it was tiresome work, so I was glad to get to Bombay at about 6.

I am at present at an Hotel, but I am going into a bungalow, which was built by Government for officers on sick leave. There are four or five of them with three rooms each. They are built on a very narrow part of the island, so there is always a nice cool sea breeze. I shall be attended by Dr. McCrimond of the 78th. whom I hear is a very nice fellow. One wing of the 78th has come here, and the other has gone to Aden, poor fellows.

Give my love to Faulk Allison, Charley Banks and Henry Iles, and remember me to all my friends. I have sent a cheque for £5 for Johnston. Will you send it to him, or send it to Uncle Kilner and ask him to pay it, but it must not reach Johnston till six weeks after you receive it, because the money will not be in Cox's hands till then. I owe him £17 but I cannot let him have it all yet. I will pay the rest as soon as I can. This trip has been expensive, and the cheque for 150 Rupees that Twemlow cashed for me will have reduced my account to a very low state."

Margaret's brother-in-law, Thomas Kilner, worked in the Bank of England, and acted as an agent and adviser both to Harry, and to William Martin in Tobago.

"You must excuse this letter, dear Mother, because it has been written at so many different times. I think my cough is rather better, and my voice a little clearer. Remember to direct my next letter to Kharrachee, Scinde. With best love to you and to Jem, Believe me ever, dear Mother, your most affectionate son, J.H.C.Loft."

In spite of Harry's optimism however, there was no improvement in his condition. He was given a thorough medical inspection on 28th November at the Colaba Depot by Dr. D.R. McCrimond, the Assistant Surgeon to the 78th Regiment, who then compiled a very detailed report:

LIEUTENANT J.H.C. LOFT

An Englishman, aged 20, complexion fair, temperament sanguineous; entered the Service in 1846, came to India with his Regiment in May 1849, and has generally enjoyed good health.

During the Monsoon, having got wet on several occasions, he was seized in September with pain in the region of the larynx and difficulty in deglutination. The inflammation spreading downwards, affected the Lungs, and a cough set in about three weeks afterwards. The cough was dry and came on in fits, generally in the mornings and evenings. On several occasions the paroxysms of coughing terminated by hemorrhages from the nose. For some days afterwards the pain in the larynx was alleviated, and the cough somewhat relieved. The cough however continued progress, and became attended with expectoration; at first of a whitish frothy character, but which gradually became thicker, of a yellowish colour, and now consists almost entirely of pus.

His chest is badly formed, the sternum projecting, the clavicular spaces flat. On expiration and inspiration the movements on both sides of the chest are performed with difficulty. Percussion over both sides tympanitic; respiration principally bronchial; about an inch above the right nipple pectoriloging is well marked; on placing the hand flat over this situation and on desiring him to speak, the parietes of the chest appear to vibrate; under both clavicles anteriorly, and posteriorly between the scapulae, there is a large resonance of voice; voice harsh and whispering; breathing hurried; dyspnoea; pulse 120, easily compressed; skin hot; tongue moist red at the tip and edges; bowels regular.

His father died of phthisis.

He is now much emaciated; suffers constantly from cough and nocturnal perspirations; is unfit for any Military Duty, and as he is making no improvement, he is therefore recommended change of climate to England. Treatment; mild expectorating remedies with counter-irritant to the chest; inhalation of steam and Iodinel.

As a result of this report Harry was given twelve months sick leave at home, from 18th December. The Earl of Balcarres was back in Bombay, preparing to sail, so his passage was booked on that ship. By this time the Regiment was in process of moving to Karrachee. Twemlow managed to pay a hurried visit to Bombay, but was unable to find Harry. He had to be content with leaving a short, very sympathetic note.

"I am vexed not to have been able to see you before the Regiment marches out. I cannot say, old chap, how devilish sorry I am that you are still on the sick list, and hope that you are soon fit enough to enjoy a bit of sport with me again. I have enjoyed having you as a companion in our joint undertakings."

The Captain of the Earl of Balcarres recognised Harry from the outward bound voyage earlier in the year, and he later said he could tell at once that Harry had come on board to die; he undoubtedly had had plenty of practice in diagnosing such cases, in view of the appalling mortality among the British Army in India. Sadly, his prediction was correct, and Harry died on 12th January 1850, a few days before his 20th birthday, and was buried at sea in the Mozambique Channel.

One of Margaret's letters must have been in the outward-bound mail ship, which passed the Earl of Balcarres on its homeward way, and she did not learn of his death until April, so she continued to write. The letters were eventually returned to her unopened two years later. Lieutenant Kirby of the 86th, who had been one of the other passengers on the Balcarres, reported Harry's death to the Adjutant General in London. After some bureaucratic delay Margaret was given official confirmation of the event, and in November 1850 was sent a cheque for 16/7d, being the balance of the pay owing to Lieutenant J.H.C.Loft, after deduction of his Mess bill, subscription to the Band, and the cost of his passage home! She also received his sword, sword belt and regimental cross-belt plate.

In July 1850 Twemlow wrote from India to Margaret in reply to a letter from her.

"I lose no time in complying with your request, and in assuring you that it will give me the greatest satisfaction in being of any assistance. Dr. Archer will write to you about his opinion of your Son's case, poor fellow. He was beloved by every officer and man in the Regiment, and we all miss him sadly as a most promising, intelligent, gentlemanly and honourable comrade. As you know, we shared a bungalow, so I had every opportunity of knowing his worth. I never met a more amiable, sweet-tempered, and gently dispositioned young man. His intelligence and honourable behaviour were remarkable.

Our communications with Bombay by water have been stopped by the Monsoon. During the stormy months all letters are sent across the desert by runners, and nothing can arrive in less than 19 days. If anything, which belonged to poor Loft, has been left in India, it must be with the Regimental Native Agent at Bombay, and I will take care that it is sent on by the one of the first ships, to the care of T. Kilner. Nothing was left with the Regiment, and there are no accounts unsettled. His pay was drawn in Bombay up to the day of his embarkation.

Before the rainy season Loft looked remarkably strong and well, and I was in great hopes that the climate of India would restore his health completely. But it was not to be. Mrs. James is writing by this Mail. I will make a point of carefully attending to every request contained in your letter, and believe me, dear Madame, yours sincerely, G. M. Twemlow.

A more unexpected tribute to Harry came in the form of some Stanzas by a an old soldier in Louth, William Evans Bactman, late of the 69th Regiment of Foot, who said that Lieutenant Loft had often visited him during his time on leave, and given him little presents. In part it reads:

Yearning for the mead of Fame,
Bent to win a trophied Name
As his sires of old had won,
Lo! the gallant youth speeds on.

Yet ere his course was well begun
Lo! that hopeful course was done,
And the wildly moaning wave
Was the youthful soldier's grave.

Harry's Roll Book

With the names and details of the men of whom he was in charge.

Alphabetical Roll of No. One Squad of Captain

Regimental No.	No. of Squad	Rank & Names.	Enlistment. Date.	Enlistment. Place.	Age at Enlist. Years.	Age at Enlist. Months	Size at Enlist Feet.	Size at Enlist Inches.	Present Size Feet.	Present Size Inches
426	1	Cr. Sergt. James Caldwell	23rd May '25	Cootehill	18	"	5	7	5	7½
1381	"	Corpl. B. T. Davidson	29 Augt. 37	Dundee	18	3	5	7½	5	8½
1991	"	Dr. Saml. McKenzie	27 Novr. '41	London	14	"	4	9½	5	5
881	"	Pte. Hugh Alexander	3rd Feb: '31	Belfast	21	"	5	6¼	5	6½
2333	"	" Louis Belson	13 May '45	Northampton	17	"	5	6½	5	6¾
691	"	" Thomas Brady	12 April '27	Cootehill	18	"	5	6	5	9½
1924	"	" William Brady	13 April '41	Limerick	18	"	5	6	5	7½
1118	"	" Thomas Browne	31 July '35	Belfast	18	"	5	6½	5	6½
1115	"	" Patrick Burke	28 July '38	do	17	6	5	6½	5	7½

Alphabetical Roll of No. One Squad of Captain

Regimental No.	No. of Squad	Rank & Names.	Enlistment. Date.	Enlistment. Place.	Age at Enlist. Years	Age at Enlist. Months	Size at Enlist Feet	Size at Enlist Inches	Present Size Feet	Present Size Inches
1273	1	Pte. Peter Clarke	2nd Aug: '36	Glasgow	18	"	5	6⅝	5	6½
2113	"	" Willm. Cleary	22 April '42	Nenagh	19	"	5	6	5	6½
2021	"	" John Coonan	23rd Septr. '42	do	20	"	5	8½	5	8½
1674	"	" Thomas Comiskey	21 May '39	Clones	18	"	5	6½	5	7
1499	"	" Denis Delory	26 May '38	Cork	17	6	5	6¼	5	7½
1401	"	" Samuel Dilly	23 Oct. '37	Dundee	19	"	5	6½	5	7¼
1871	"	" Charles Duffey	20 May '40	Boyle	20	"	5	–¾	5	7¾
2283	"	" Joseph Duffey	5 March '44	do	18	"	5	6⅜	5	6½
641	"	" Patrick Duffy	5 March '26	Carrick on Suir	17	"	5	6½	5	8
1383	"	" Peter Emslie	1st Sepr. '37	Dundee	21	"	5	7	5	7¼

G. C. B. Stirling's Company, in Charge of Cr. Sergeant J. Caldwell

Country.	Religion.	Trade.	Married. Leave	Married. Without	No. of Children Boys.	No. of Children Girls.	In Barracks	No. of Arms	No. of Gt.Coats	Date of Great Coat.	No. of Cts. Martials Regtal.	No. of Cts. Martials Dist.	No. of Cts. Martials General	Remarks.
I	P	Labourer	1	"	2	1	Yes	1	1	Septr. 1843	"	"	"	
S	P	Clerk	1	"	"	"	"	1	1	do	1	"	"	P. G. C. Pay
I	P	Tailor	"	"	"	"	"	"	1	do	"	"	"	
I	P	Labourer	"	"	"	"	"	53			"	"	"	2d. Addl. Pay
E	P	do	"	"	"	"	"	59	59	Septr. 1843	"	"	"	
I	C	do	1	"	2	1	No	6	6	do	1	"	"	2d Addl. Pay
I	P	Clerk	"	1	1	"	"	54	42	do	"	"	"	
I	P	Labourer	"	"	"	"	Yes	7	7	do	"	"	"	1 G. C. B.
I	C	do	"	1	"	"	No	8	8	do	"	"	"	

G. C. B. Stirling's Company, in Charge of Cr. Sergt. J. Caldwell.

Country.	Religion,	Trade	Married Leave	Married Without	No of Children Boys	No of Children Girls	In Barracks	No. of Arms	No. of Gt. Coats	Date of Great Coat.	No. of Cts. Martial Regtal.	No. of Cts. Martial Dist.	No. of Cts. Martial General	Remarks.
I	C	Labourer	"	"	"	"	Yes	10	10	Septr. 1843	"	"	"	
I	C	do	"	"	"	"	"	56	6	do	"	"	"	
I	C	do	"	"	"	"	"	55	43	1st June 1842	1	"	"	
I	C	do	"	"	"	"	"	12	12	Septr. 1843	"	"	"	
I	C	do	"	1	1	"	No	13	13	do	"	"	"	
I	P	Weaver	"	"	"	"	Yes	14	14	do	"	"	"	
I	C	Labourer	"	"	"	"	"	16	16	do	"	"	"	
I	C	do	"	"	"	"	"	65	40	do	"	"	"	
I	C	do	"	1	1	"	No	15	15	do	1	1	"	2d. Addl. Pay.
S	P	Flaxdresser	"	"	"	"	Yes	17	17	do	"	"	"	

Alphabetical Roll of No. One Squad —— of Captain

	Regimental No.	No. of Squad	Rank & Names	Enlistment Date	Enlistment Place	Age at Enlist. Years	Age at Enlist. Months	Size at Enlist Feet	Size at Enlist Inches	Present Size Feet	Present Size Inches
12	1630	1	Pte. James Falloon	2d April '39	Londonderry	20	"	5	6¼	5	6¼
2	2124	"	" James Farmer	9 April '42	Coventry	17	3	5	5⅞	5	5¼
2	472	"	" John Feely	25 Septr. '25	Ballyshannon	21	"	5	6¾	5	6½
1	~~2328~~	"	"								

Alphabetical Roll of ~~No.~~ the Left Subdivision of Captain

Regimental No.	No. of Squad	Rank & Names	Enlistment Date	Enlistment Place	Age at Enlist. Years	Age at Enlist. Months	Size at Enlist Feet	Size at Enlist Inches	Present Size Feet	Present Size Inches
		Sergeant								
1032	3	James Howel	5 Octr. 33	Swafflam	18	"	5	7¼	5	7½
		Corporal								
1564	3	John Hagherty	10 Decr. '38	Derry	18	"	5	6¾	5	7
		Privates								
1802	3	Thomas Lavin	4 Jany. '40	Boyle	18	"	5	7¾	5	9¼
689	3	John Little (1 [illegible])	31 Mar '27	Cootehill	18	"	5	5½	5	6

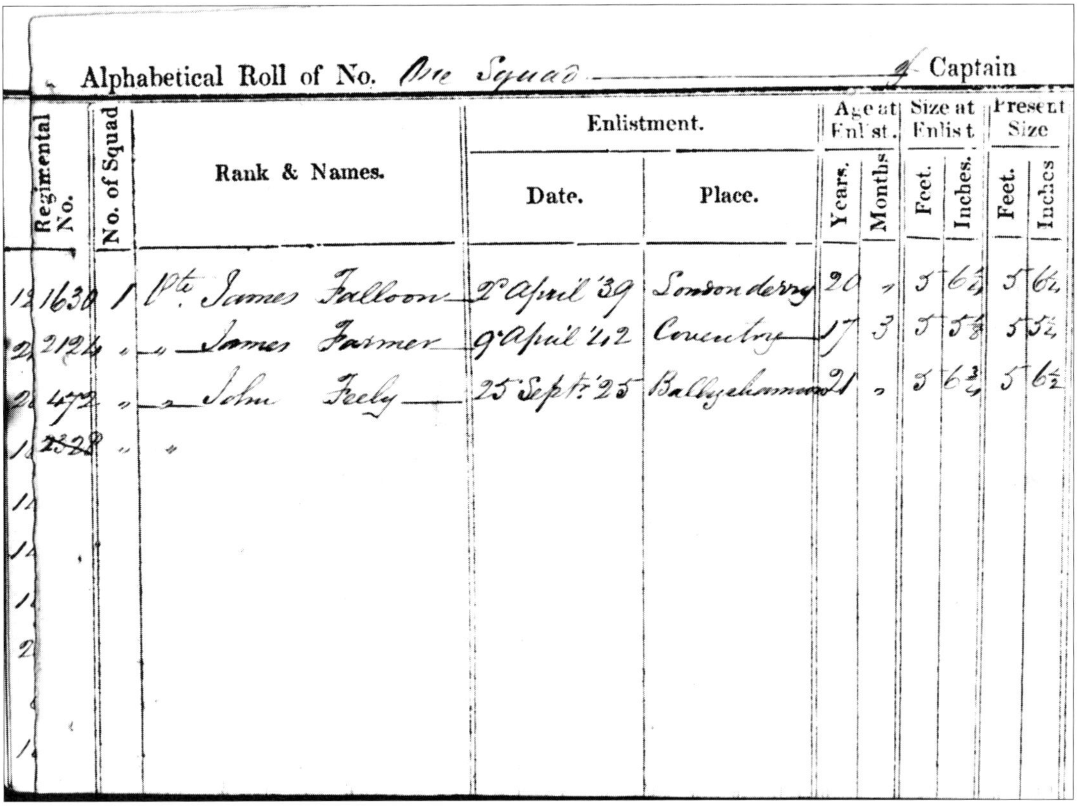

Alphabetical Roll of No. One Squad ——— of Captain

Regimental No.	No. of Squad	Rank & Names	Enlistment. Date.	Enlistment. Place.	Age at Enlist. Years.	Age at Enlist. Months	Size at Enlist. Feet.	Size at Enlist. Inches.	Present Size Feet.	Present Size Inches
1630	1	Pte. James Falloon	2d April '39	Londonderry	20	"	5	6½	5	6½
2124	"	" James Farmer	9 April '42	Coventry	17	3	5	5⅞	5	5½
472	"	" John Feely	25 Sept. '25	Ballyshannon	21	"	5	6¾	5	6½
~~2328~~	"	"								

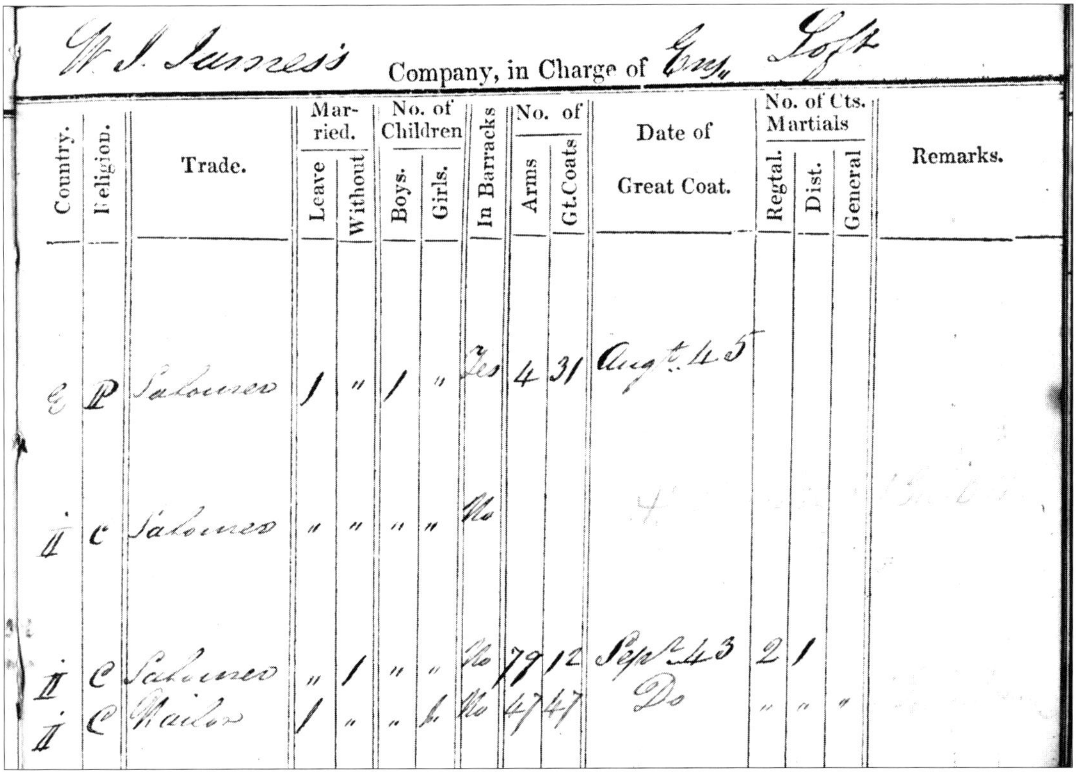

W. J. Sumner's Company, in Charge of Ens. Loft

Country.	Religion.	Trade.	Married. Leave	Married. Without	No. of Children Boys.	No. of Children Girls.	In Barracks	No. of Arms	No. of Gt.Coats	Date of Great Coat.	No. of Cts. Martials Regtal.	Dist.	General	Remarks.
E	P	Labourer	1	"	1	"	Yes	4	31	Augt. 45				
I	C	Labourer	"	"	"	"	No							
I	C	Labourer	"	1	"	"	No	79	12	Sept. 43	2	1		
I	C	Tailor	1	"	"	1	No	47	47	Do	"	"	"	

Continued
Alphabetical Roll of ~~No.~~ the Left Subdivision of Captain

Regimental No.	No. of Squad	Rank & Names	Enlistment Date	Enlistment Place	Age at Enlist. Years	Age at Enlist. Months	Size at Enlist Feet	Size at Enlist Inches	Present Size Feet	Present Size Inches
		Privates								
2400	3	John Little 2nd	4 Feb 46	Dublin	17	"	5	5¾	5	6
2391	3	John Lock	31 Decr 45	Exeter	17	11	5	6¼	5	6½
566	3	William Loram	6 Jany 26	Ashburton	26	"	5	6	5	6½
1201	3	John Lyon	21 Sept 35	Edinburgh	18	3	5	6⅛	5	7
1705	3	William McAnulty	26 July 39	Sligo	18	"	5	6¼	5	8
1034	3	Thomas McClunkin	10 Novr 33	Ballymena	20	"	5	6½	5	7½
2216	3	Daniel McCormick	20 Sept 42	Glasgow	20	"	5	8¼	5	9

Continued
Alphabetical Roll of ~~No.~~ the Left Subdivision of Captain

Regimental No.	No. of Squad	Rank & Names	Enlistment Date	Enlistment Place	Age at Enlist. Years	Age at Enlist. Months	Size at Enlist Feet	Size at Enlist Inches	Present Size Feet	Present Size Inches
		Privates								
1704	3	James McCormick	26 July 39	Sligo	20	"	5	10	5	10
1536	3	James McDermott	29 Octr 38	Belfast	18	"	5	6¼	5	8
2410	3	Archibald McDonald	27 Novr 44	Ballymoney	17	8	5	6¼	5	7
1304	3	Donald McDonald	19 Decr 36	Fort George	17	6	5	6¼	5	8
1303	3	Neill McDonald	17 Novr 36	Glasgow	18	"	5	6	5	6½
2408	3	John McGlynn	26 June 46	Belturbet	18	"	5	6½	5	6½
2060	3	Charles McGranaghan	2 Mar 42	Edinburgh	17	"	5	5½	5	6
2159	3	Robert McGregor	20 May 42	Do	19	"	5	6	5	6
1235	3	George McLaughlin	24 Feb 36	Glasgow	18	"	5	6½	5	6¾

W. J. James's Company, in Charge of Ens. Loft

Country.	Religion.	Trade	Married: Leave	Married: Without	No. of Children: Boys	No. of Children: Girls	In Barracks	No. of: Arms	No. of: Gt. Coats	Date of Great Coat.	No. of Cts. Martial: Regtal.	No. of Cts. Martial: Dist.	No. of Cts. Martial: General	Remarks.
I	P	Groom	"	"	"	"	Yes	80	57	Sept. 43				
E	P	Labourer	"	"	"	"	"	57	51	Do				
E	P	Do	"	1	"	"	No	48	48	Do				
I	C	Do	"	"	"	"	Yes	7	1	Augt. 45	2	"	"	
I	C	Do	"	"	"	"	"	31	36	Sept. 43				
I	P	Do	"	1	"	2	No	23	23	Do				
S	P	Mason	"	"	"	"	Yes	4	27	Augt. 45	"	1	"	

W. J. James's Company, in Charge of Ens. Loft

Country.	Religion.	Trade.	Married: Leave	Married: Without	No. of Children: Boys.	No. of Children: Girls.	In Barracks	No. of: Arms	No. of: Gt. Coats	Date of Great Coat.	No. of Cts. Martials: Regtal.	No. of Cts. Martials: Dist.	No. of Cts. Martials: General	Remarks.
I	C	Labourer	"	"	"	"	Yes	51	71	Augt. 45				
I	P	Do	"	"	"	"	"	73	73	Do				
I	C	Butcher	"	"	"	"	"	33	14	Sept. 43				
S	P	Shoe Maker	"	"	"	"	"	42	59	Do	1	"	"	
S	P	Weaver	1	"	"	1	No	2	2	Do	1	"	"	
I	C	Labourer	"	"	"	"	Yes	19	10	Do				
I	C	Do	"	"	"	"	"	64	34	Augt. 45	"	1	"	
S	P	Clerk	"	"	"	"	"	56	32	Do	"	"	"	
I	C	Labourer	1	"	1	"	No	18	3	Sept. 43	1	"	"	

Alphabetical Roll of No. the Left Subdivision Captain

Regimental	Regimental No.	No. of Squad	Rank & Names	Enlistment. Date.	Enlistment. Place.	Age at Enlist. Years	Age at Enlist. Months	Size at Enlist Feet	Size at Enlist Inches	Present Size Feet	Present Size Inches
			Sergeant								
21	1181	4	Patrick Reilly	16 Sept 35	Enniskillen	18	"	5	7 3/4	5	8 1/2
			Corporals								
	1604	4	James Wilson	10 Jan 39	Glasgow	18	"	5	7	5	7 1/2
			Privates								
	2185	4	John Meagher	30 July 42	Nenagh	17	6	5	6	5	6
	489	4	William Mills	12 Octr 25	Cootehill	18	"	5	5 1/2	5	8 1/2
	1532	4	Daniel Monaghan	2 Augt 38	Newry	18	"	5	7	5	9 1/2

Continued Alphabetical Roll of No. Left Subdivision of Captain

Regimental No.	No. of Squad	Rank & Names	Enlistment. Date.	Enlistment. Place.	Age at Enlist. Years	Age at Enlist. Months	Size at Enlist Feet	Size at Enlist Inches	Present Size Feet	Present Size Inches
		Privates								
1505	4	John Mullin	30 June 38	Derry	18	"	5	6 1/2	5	8
2249	4	George Murphy	11 Jan 39	Dublin	19	"	5	8 1/2	5	8 1/2
1804	4	James Murray	16 Jan 40	Boyle	17	"	5	5 1/4	5	6 1/4
2002	4	John Paul	11 Decr 41	Ballamana	21	"	5	6 1/4	5	6 1/2
2426	4	William Peacock	17 Feb 46	Macclesfield	17	6	5	6 3/4	5	7
670	4	Michael Reilly	10 Feb 27	Cootehill	19	"	5	7	5	8

W. S. James's Company, in Charge of Ens. Loft

Country.	Religion.	Trade.	Married. Leave	Married. Without	No. of Children Boys.	No. of Children Girls.	In Barracks	No. of Arms	No. of Gt. Coats	Date of Great Coat.	No. of Cts. Martials Regtal.	No. of Cts. Martials Dist.	No. of Cts. Martials General	Remarks.
I	C	Labourer	"	"	"	"	Yes	3	3	Septr 43				
S	P	Labourer	"	"	"	"	Yes	44	64	Septr 43				
I	C	Labourer	"	"	"	"	Yes	58	57	Augt 45				
I	P	Do	1	"	"	"	No	53	47	Septr 43	1	2	"	
I	C	Do	"	"	"	"	Yes	28	7	Do	1	"	"	

W. S. James's Company, in Charge of Ens. Loft

Country.	Religion.	Trade.	Married. Leave	Married. Without	No. of Children Boys.	No. of Children Girls.	In Barracks	No. of Arms	No. of Gt. Coats	Date of Great Coat.	No. of Cts. Martials Regtal.	No. of Cts. Martials Dist.	No. of Cts. Martials General	Remarks.
I	P	Labourer	"	1	"	"	No	60	60	Septr 43	"	"	"	
I	C	Do	1	"	"	1	No	61	61	Augt 45	"	"	"	
I	C	Do	"	1	"	1	No	63	63	Septr 43	1	"	"	
I	P	Shoe Maker	"	"	"	"	Yes	65	67	Septr 43	"	2	"	
E	P	Silk Weaver	"	"	"	"	"	36	46	Do	"	"	"	
I	C	Weaver	"	"	1	1	Yes	66	66	Do	"	"	"	

Continued

Alphabetical Roll of ~~No.~~ Left Subdivision of Captain

Regimental No.	No. of Squad	Rank & Names	Enlistment Date	Enlistment Place	Age at Enlist. Years	Age at Enlist. Months	Size at Enlist Feet	Size at Enlist Inches	Present Size Feet	Present Size Inches
		Privates								
2095	4	John Russell	23 Mar 42	Glasgow	18	"	5	5½	5	5¾
1974	4	William Slattery	29 Octr 41	Templemore	18	"	5	6¼	5	7¼
2327	4	Andrew Sleator	12 Mar 45	Shercock	18	"	5	6½	5	7
1350	4	Robert Smith	2 Augt 37	Dundee	18	"	5	6¼	5	7
2263	4	James Somers	7 Septr 43	Portsmouth	15	9	4	10½	5	3
653	4	Robert Somers	17 Mar 26	Carlow	23	"	5	7½	5	7½

Continued

Alphabetical Roll of ~~No.~~ the Left Subdivision of Captain

Regimental No.	No. of Squad	Rank & Names	Enlistment Date	Enlistment Place	Age at Enlist. Years	Age at Enlist. Months	Size at Enlist Feet	Size at Enlist Inches	Present Size Feet	Present Size Inches
		Privates								
2434	4	William Southwood	20 Feb 46	Barnstaple	17	11	5	5½	5	5½
877	4	Thomas Stewart	27 Jany 31	Belfast	19	"	5	7½	5	7½
2220	4	Hugh Sweeney	6 July 42	Glasgow	20	"	5	8¼	5	9
1860	4	John Tregillis	16 Septr 39	Devonport	18	"	5	6	5	6

W. S. James's Company, in Charge of Ens. Loft

Country.	Religion,	Trade	Married: Leave	Married: Without	No of Children: Boys	No of Children: Girls	In Barracks	No of: Arms	No of: Gt. Coats	Date of Great Coat.	No. of Cts. Martial: Regtal.	No. of Cts. Martial: Dist.	No. of Cts. Martial: General	Remarks.
S	P	Labourer	"	1	1	"	No	68	68	Sepr. 43				
I	C	Tailor	"	"	"	"	Yes	16	20	Do	"	1	"	
I	P	Do	"	"	"	"	"	29	25	Augt 45				
S	P	Weaver	"	"	"	"	"	74	74	Sepr. 43	"	1	"	
I	C	None	"	"	"	"	"	"	80	Do				
I	C	Labourer	1	"	3	1	No	72	72	Do				[illegible]

W. S. James's Company, in Charge of Ens. Loft

Country.	Religion,	Trade	Married: Leave	Married: Without	No of Children: Boys	No of Children: Girls	In Barracks	No. of: Arms	No. of: Gt. Coats	Date of Great Coat.	No. of Cts. Martial: Regtal.	No. of Cts. Martial: Dist.	No. of Cts. Martial: General	Remarks.
E	P	Labourer	"	"	"	"	Yes	77	26	Augt 45	"	"	"	
I	P	Weaver	"	"	"	"	"	1	75	Sepr. 43	1	"	"	
S	P	Labourer	"	"	"	"	"	76	69	April 45	1	1	"	
E	P	Shoe Maker	"	"	.	.	"	78	78	Sepr. 43	"	"	"	

Alphabetical Roll of No. Left Subdivision Captain

Regimental No.	No. of Squad	Rank & Names.	Enlistment. Date.	Enlistment. Place.	Age at Enlist. Years	Age at Enlist. Months	Size at Enlist Feet.	Size at Enlist Inches.	Present Size Feet.	Present Size Inches
926		Serg^t R H Echlin	4th Novr 31	Belfast	18	"	5	8	5	9½
966		" W^m McDonald	29 Mar 32	London	14	"	4	6½	5	10¼
2379		Corp^l J^s Walker	19 Novr 45	Dublin	17	"	5	6½	5	9
1927		" St Wilson	23 Apl 41	Limerick	16	"	5	3	5	6¾
1923		Dr John Wilson	2 Apl 41	Limerick	14	9	4	10	5	4¾
		— Privates —								
2114		William Lithgow	4 April 42	Newry	18	"	5	5½	5	6½
2391		John Lock	31 Dec 45	Exeter	17	11	5	6¼	5	6¾
2558		Peter Lynagh	21 Jan 47	Cahir	18	"	5	8	5	8½
2919		Richard McCann	8 Dec 48	Thurles	18	"	5	6	5	6

Alphabetical Roll of No. Left Subdivision Captain

Regimental No.	No. of Squad	Rank & Names.	Enlistment. Date.	Enlistment. Place.	Age at Enlist. Years	Age at Enlist. Months	Size at Enlist Feet	Size at Enlist Inches	Present Size Feet	Present Size Inches
1405		William McCarter	27 Octr 37	Dundee	22	"	5	8½	5	7¾
1511		John McConnell	18 June 38	Belfast	21	"	5	7½	5	7½
2532		Denis McDonald	2 June 47	Templemore	18	"	5	8½	5	8¼
1893		John McDonald	22 Mar 39	Scarva	20	"	5	5¾	5	5½
1612		Mich^l McGinley	22 Feb 39	L. Derry	18	"	5	6½	5	7¼
2062		John McGonegal	14 Mar 42	Glasgow	20	"	5	6⅞	5	6½
1319		John McNamara	20 Dec 36	Glasgow	19	"	5	8⅞	5	9½
1534		James McMullin	21 Aug 31	L. Derry	18	"	5	7	5	1½
2894		Geo. Matthews	18 Nov 48	Stafford	21	"	5	6½	5	6
1532		Daniel Monaghan	2 Octr 38	Newry	18	"	5	7	5	8¾

C. Pattisons Company, in Charge of Lieut Loft

Country.	Religion.	Trade.	Married. Leave	Married. Without	No. of Children Boys.	No. of Children Girls.	In Barracks	No. of Arms	No. of Gt.Coats	Date of ~~Great Coat.~~ Joining	No. of Cts. Martials Regtal.	Dist.	General	Remarks. In. India
I	P	Labourer	"	"	"	"	"	2	2	11 Novr. 31	1	"	"	25 May 49
E	P	None	1	"	"	1	"	4	4	22 Apl. 32	"	"	"	17 — do
I	P	Labourer	"	"	"	"	"	82	82	21 Novr. 45	"	"	"	2 June 47
I	P	None	1	"	"	1	"	4	4	24 Apl. 41	"	"	"	17 May 49
I	P	None	"	"	"	"	"	2	2	3 Apl. 41	"	"	"	17 — do
I	P	Printer	"	"	"	"	"	42	42	21 Apl. 42	"	"	"	17 do
E	P	Labourer	1	"	"	"	"	87	87	12 Jany. 46	"	"	"	17 do
I	C	Labourer	"	"	"	"	"	58	58	2 Feb. 47	"	"	"	17 do
I	C	Labourer	"	"	"	"	"	23	23	20 Decr. 48	"	"	"	17 do

C. Pattisons Company, in Charge of Lieut Loft

Country.	Religion.	Trade.	Married. Leave	Married. Without	No. of Children Boys.	No. of Children Girls.	In Barracks	No. of Arms	No. of Gt.Coats	Date of ~~Great Coat.~~ Joining	No. of Cts. Martials Regtal.	Dist.	General	Remarks. In. India
S	P	Labourer	1	"	1	1	"	24	24	30 Oct. 37	"	1	"	17 May 1849
I	C	Labourer	"	"	"	"	"	46	46	10 July 38		1	"	17 do
I	C	Labourer	"	"	"	"	"	43	43	8 June 47	"	"	"	17 — do
I	C	Labourer	"	1	"	1	"	49	49	1 Sept. 40	"	"	"	17 do
I	C	Labourer	"	"	"	"	"	57	57	23 Feb. 39	2	"	"	18 — do
I	P	Labourer	"	"	"	"	"	57		30 Mar. 42	"	4	"	17 — do
I	C	Labourer	"	"	"	"	"	6	6	28 Jany. 37				4 — do
I	C	Labourer	"	"	"	"	"			23 Augt. 38	1	4	"	17 — do
E	P	Labourer	"	"	"	"	"	48	48	19 Decr. 46	"	"	"	17 — do
I	C	Labourer	"	"	"	"	"	89	89	19 Augt. 38				17 — do

Alphabetical Roll of No. Left Subdivision Captain

Regimental No.	No. of Squad	Rank & Names.	Enlistment. Date.	Enlistment. Place.	Age at Enlist. Years	Age at Enlist. Months	Size at Enlist Feet	Size at Enlist Inches	Present Size Feet	Present Size Inches
1104		Patrick Moran	28 May 35	Castlebar	20	"	5	7	5	6¾
2771		Charles Moore	8 Sepr 48	Belfast	17	6	5	6¼	5	7
2983		James Mullamphy	14 Decr 48	Dublin	18	"	5	6	5	5½
1361		Samuel Murray	24th April 37	Glasgow	16	6	5	6¾	5	7¾
2571		Michl O'Brien 1st	26 Octr 47	Limerick	21	"	5	7	5	6¾
2956		Michl O'Brien 2nd	19 Decr 48	Cork	19	"	5	6¾	5	7¼
2886		John O'Callaghan	1 Decr 48	Limerick	19	"	5	8½	5	8¼
2708		Joseph Ottler	25 July 48	Stow Market	19	"	5	6½	5	7¼
2626		Geo. Parnell	14 Febr 48	Leicester	19	3	5	6½	5	7
2002		John Paul	11 Decr 41	Ballymena	21	"	5	6¼	5	6
1613		Robert Pearson	22 Feby 39	L. Derry	18	"	5	6½	5	6

Alphabetical Roll of No. Left Subdivision Captain

Regimental No.	No. of Squad	Rank & Names.	Enlistment. Date.	Enlistment. Place.	Age at Enlist. Years.	Age at Enlist. Months	Size at Enlist Feet.	Size at Enlist Inches.	Present Size Feet.	Present Size Inches
2755		Frederick Randall	12 Octr 48	Leicester	19	3	5	6½	5	7
1520		James Rennie	3 July 38	Belfast	18	"	5	6¼	5	7¼
2517		Charles Rice	22 Feby 47	Kilkenny	18	6	5	6¾	5	6½
1865		William Robinson	16 April 40	Belfast	18	"	5	5¼	5	6½
2838		Patrick Ryan 1st	18 Novr 48	Ballina	22	7	5	8	5	7¾
2868		Patrick Ryan 2nd	6 Decr 48	Limerick	20	"	5	6½	5	5¾
2699		Geo. Ryall	11 July 48	Leicester	17	11	5	6¼	5	6½
2417		William Shaddick	3 Feby 46	Bideford	17	11	5	5¾	5	7
1202		Henry Simpson	3 Oct 35	Edinburgh	22	1	5	8¼	5	9
2470		William Simmons	10 July 46	Barnstaple	17	9	5	5¾	5	7¼

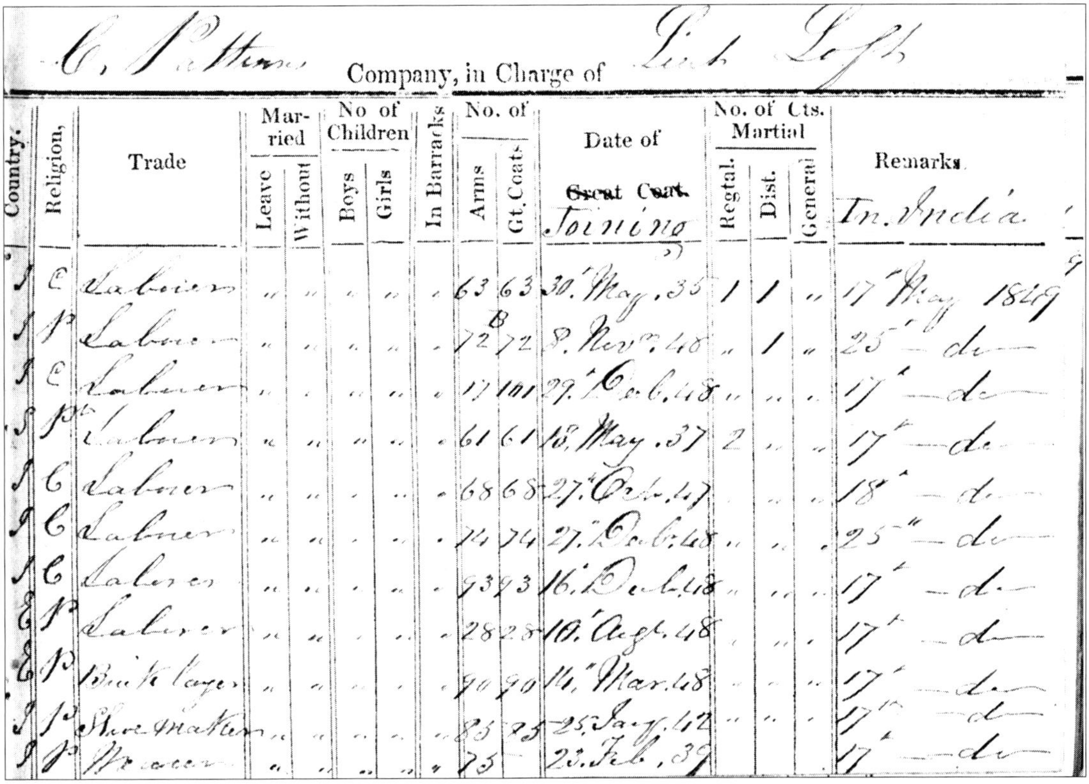

C. Pattisons Company, in Charge of Lieut Loft

Country.	Religion,	Trade	Married: Leave	Married: Without	No of Children: Boys	No of Children: Girls	In Barracks	No. of: Arms	No. of: Gt. Coats	Date of ~~Great Coat.~~ Joining	No. of Cts. Martial: Regtal.	No. of Cts. Martial: Dist.	No. of Cts. Martial: General	Remarks. In India
I	C	Labourer	"	"	"	"	"	63	63	30th May. 35	1	1	"	17th May 1849
I	P	Labourer	"	"	"	"	"	72	72	8. Novr. 48	"	1	"	25th do
I	C	Labourer	"	"	"	"	"	17	101	29th Decb. 48	"	"	"	17th do
S	Pt	Labourer	"	"	"	"	"	61	61	18. May. 37	2	"	"	17th do
I	C	Labourer	"	"	"	"	"	68	68	27th Octr. 47		"	"	18th do
I	C	Labourer	"	"	"	"	"	74	74	27th Decbr. 48	"	"	"	25th do
I	C	Labourer	"	"	"	"	"	93	93	16. Decb. 48	"	"	"	17th do
E	P	Labourer	"	"	"	"	"	28	28	10th Augt. 48		"	"	17th do
E	P	Bricklayer	"	"	"	"	"	90	90	14th Mar. 48		"	"	17th do
I	P	Shoemaker	"	"	"	"	"	85	85	25. Jany. 42	"	"	"	17th do
I	P	Weaver	"	"	"	"	"	75		23. Feb. 39				17th do

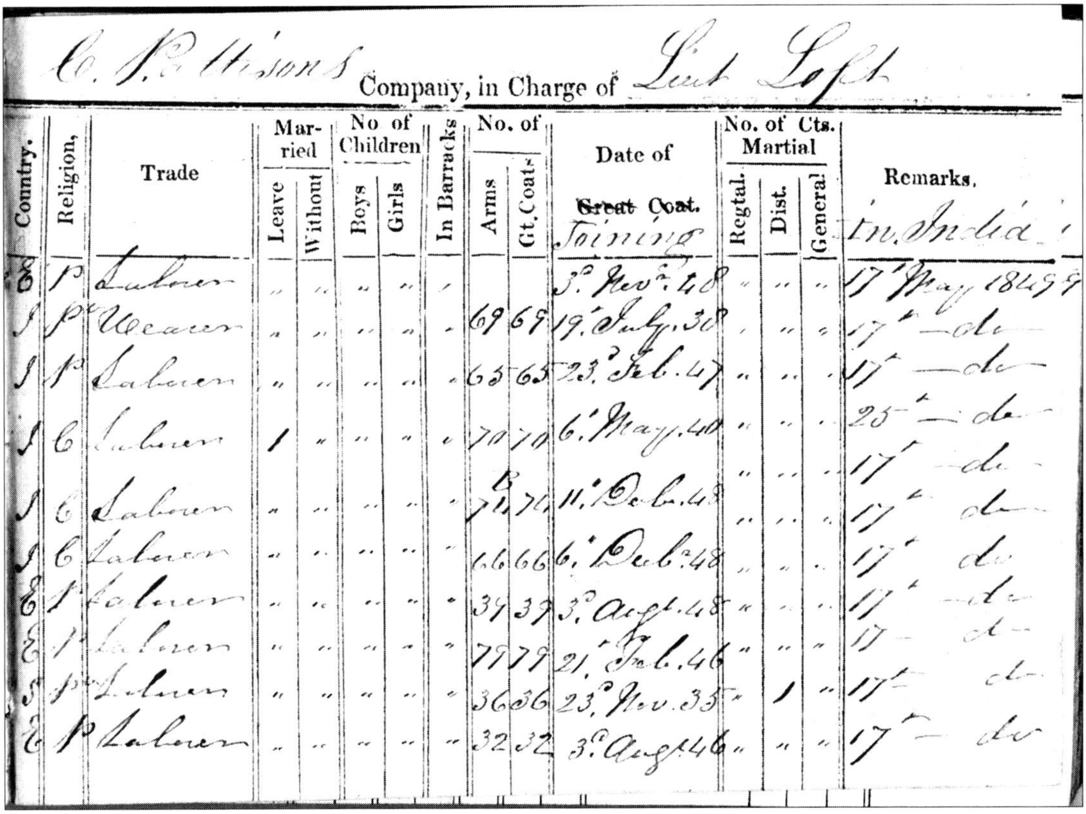

C. P. Pattisons Company, in Charge of Lieut Loft

Country.	Religion,	Trade	Married: Leave	Married: Without	No of Children: Boys	No of Children: Girls	In Barracks	No. of: Arms	No. of: Gt. Coats	Date of ~~Great Coat.~~ Joining	No. of Cts. Martial: Regtal.	No. of Cts. Martial: Dist.	No. of Cts. Martial: General	Remarks. in India
S	P	Labourer	"	"	"	"	"			3d Novr. 48	"	"	"	17th May 1849
I	Pt	Weaver	"	"	"	"	"	69	69	19th July. 38	"	"	"	17th do
I	P	Labourer	"	"	"	"	"	65	65	23d Feb. 47	"	"	"	17th do
I	C	Labourer	1	"	"	"	"	70	70	6th May. 40	"	"	"	25th do
											"	"	"	17th do
I	C	Labourer	"	"	"	"	"	74	74	11th Decb. 48	"	"	"	17th do
I	C	Labourer	"	"	"	"	"	66	66	6th Decbr. 48	"	"	"	17th do
E	P	Labourer	"	"	"	"	"	39	39	3d Augt. 48	"	"	"	17th do
E	P	Labourer	"	"	"	"	"	77	77	21st Feb. 46	"	"	"	17th do
S	Pt	Labourer	"	"	"	"	"	36	36	23d Nov. 35	"	1	"	17th do
E	P	Labourer	"	"	"	"	"	32	32	3d Augt. 46	"	"	"	17th do

Alphabetical Roll of No. *Left Subdivision* Captain

Regimental No.	No. of Squad	Rank & Names.	Enlistment. Date.	Enlistment. Place.	Age at Enl'st. Years.	Age at Enl'st. Months	Size at Enlist Feet.	Size at Enlist Inches.	Present Size Feet.	Present Size Inches
2755		Frederick Randall	12 Octr 48	Leicester	19	3	5	6½	5	7
1520		James Rennie	3d July 38	Belfast	18	"	5	6¼	5	7¼
2517		Charles Rice	22d Feb 47	Killkenny	18	6	5	6¾	5	6½
1865		William Robinson	16 April 40	Belfast	18	"	5	5¼	5	6½
2838		Patrick Ryan 1st	18 Novr 48	Ballina	22	7	5	8	5	7¾
2860		Patrick Ryan 2d	6 Decr 48	Limerick	20	"	5	6¼	5	5¾
2699		Geo. Ryall	11 July 48	Leicester	17	11	5	6¼	5	6½
2417		William Shaddick	3 Feby 46	Bideford	17	11	5	5¾	5	7
1202		Henry Simpson	3d Oct 35	Edinburgh	22	1	5	8¼	5	9
2470		William Simmons	10 July 46	Barnstaple	17	9	5	5¾	5	7¼

Alphabetical Roll of No. *Left Subdivision* Captain

Regimental No.	No. of Squad	Rank & Names.	Enlistment. Date.	Enlistment. Place.	Age at Enl'st. Years.	Age at Enl'st. Months	Size at Enlist Feet.	Size at Enlist Inches.	Present Size Feet.	Present Size Inches
2941		Geo. Smith	15 Decr 48	Liverpool	19	"	5	6½	5	6
2780		Joseph Smith	20 Octr 48	Halifax	17	"	5	6¾	5	7½
2112		William Smith	9 Mar 42	Halifax N.S.	16	10	5	1	5	7½
2222		William Spring	12 Novr 42	Tralee	17	"	5	5½	5	6¾
1265		John Stark	18 June 36	Glasgow	18	3	5	6½	5	7½
2263		James Sommers	7 Sept 43	Falmouth	15	9	4	10½	5	8
2862		Robert Stevens	5 Decr 48	Limerick	20	"	5	7¼	5	6½
2460		Geo. Street	5 Octr 46	Nottingham	17	"	5	5	5	5¾
2228		William Virtue	4 Octr 41	Glasgow	17	"	5	6¼	5	7
2787		Patrick Wall	24 Novr 48	Clonmel	18	"	5	6	5	6

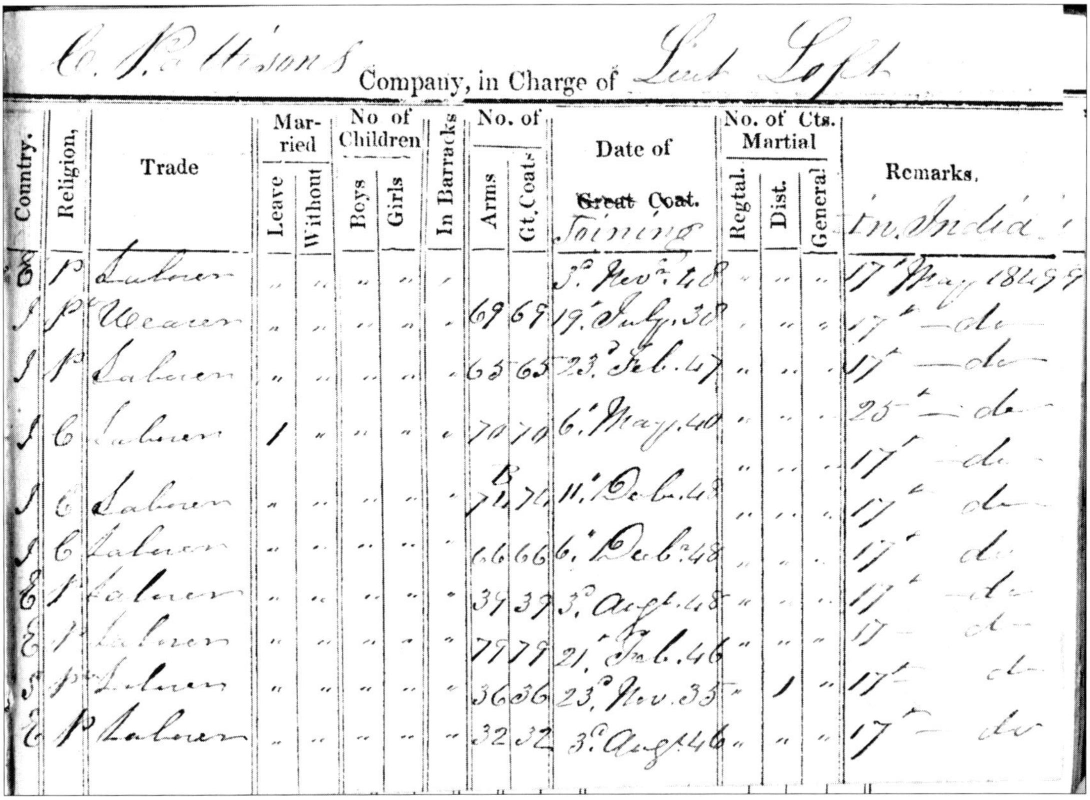

C. Pattison's Company, in Charge of Lieut Loft

Country.	Religion.	Trade	Married: Leave	Married: Without	No of Children: Boys	No of Children: Girls	In Barracks	No. of: Arms	No. of: Gt. Coats	Date of Great Coat. Joining	No. of Cts. Martial: Regtal.	Dist.	General	Remarks. In India
S	P	Labourer	"	"	"	"	"			3d Nov. 48	"	"	"	17 May 1849
I	Pt	Weaver	"	"	"	"	"	69	69	19. July. 30	"	"	"	17th do
I	P	Labourer	"	"	"	"	"	65	65	23. Feb. 47	"	"	"	17th do
I	C	Labourer	1	"	"	"	"	70	70	6. May. 40	"	"	"	25th do
I	C	Labourer	"	"	"	"	"	B 71	70	11. Dec. 48	"	"	"	17th do
I	C	Labourer	"	"	"	"	"	66	66	6. Dec. 48	"	"	"	17th do
E	P	Labourer	"	"	"	"	"	39	39	3d Aug. 48	"	"	"	17th do
E	P	Labourer	"	"	"	"	"	77	77	21st Feb. 46	"	"	"	17th do
S	Pt	Labourer	"	"	"	"	"	36	36	23d Nov. 35	"	1	"	17th do
E	P	Labourer	"	"	"	"	"	32	32	3d Aug. 46	"	"	"	17th do

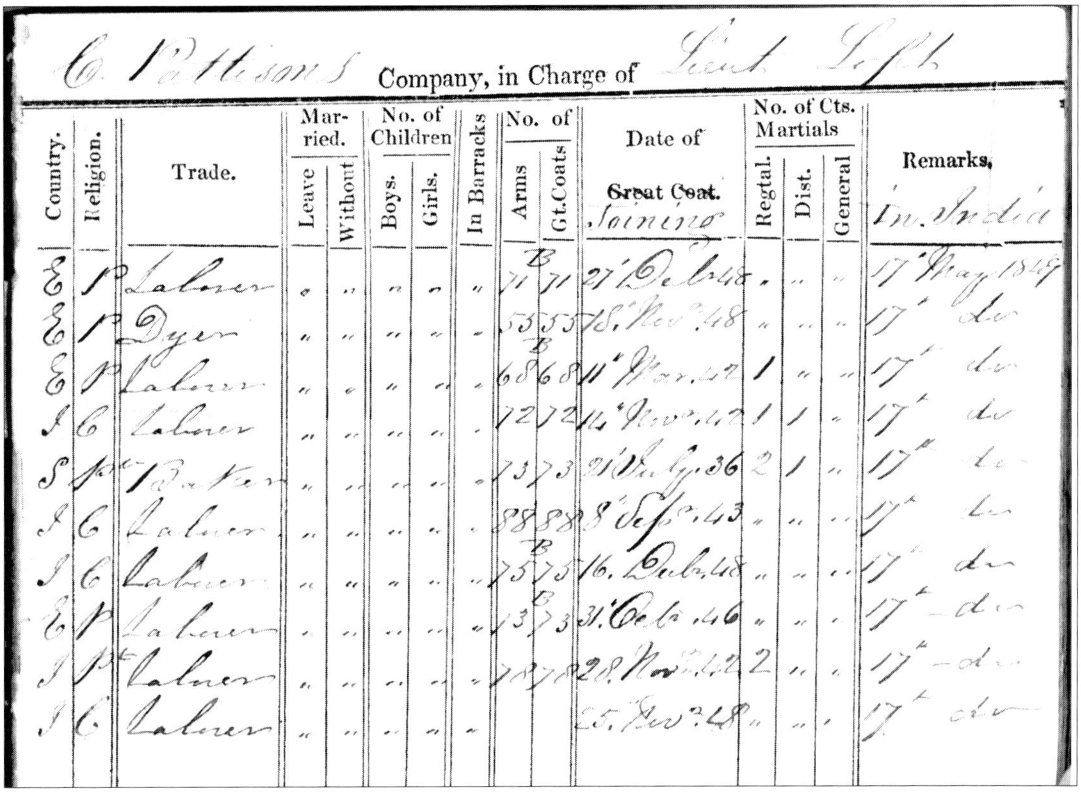

C. Pattison's Company, in Charge of Lieut Loft

Country.	Religion.	Trade.	Married: Leave	Married: Without	No. of Children: Boys.	No. of Children: Girls.	In Barracks	No. of: Arms	No. of: Gt. Coats	Date of Great Coat. Joining	No. of Cts. Martials: Regtal.	Dist.	General	Remarks. In India
E	P	Labourer	"	"	"	"	"	B 71	71	27 Dec. 48	"	"	"	17 May 1849
E	P	Dyer	"	"	"	"	"	55	55	18 Nov. 48	"	"	"	17th do
E	P	Labourer	"	"	"	"	"	B 68	68	11 Mar. 42	1	"	"	17th do
I	C	Labourer	"	"	"	"	"	72	72	14 Nov. 42	1	1	"	17th do
S	Pt	Baker	"	"	"	"	"	73	73	21 July. 36	2	1	"	17th do
I	C	Labourer	"	"	"	"	"	88	88	8 Sep. 43	"	"	"	17th do
I	C	Labourer	"	"	"	"	"	B 75	75	16. Dec. 48	"	"	"	17th do
E	P	Labourer	"	"	"	"	"	B 73	73	31. Dec. 46	"	"	"	17th do
I	Pt	Labourer	"	"	"	"	"	78	78	28. Nov. 42	2	"	"	17th do
I	C	Labourer	"	"	"	"	"			25. Nov. 48	"	"	"	17th do

INDIAN TEMPLES C.1850

CHAPTER 11

EPILOGUE

It is almost impossible to imagine how Margaret reacted to this last tragic blow, especially when she learned that her brother William Martin had died in Tobago a fortnight after Harry's death, aged 33. After Dr. Smith's warnings, when Harry had been ill in Ireland, it seems unlikely that Margaret can have been in any doubt of the precarious nature of his health. She could not help expressing her anxiety about him, but she was always careful in her letters to avoid saying anything that might alarm Harry unduly.

From the evidence of their letters it would appear that the relationship between herself and Harry had been a specially close one, almost as if they had been good friends, rather than mother and son. She had always confided in him everything that was in her mind, and had consulted him over all sorts of decisions that confronted her, even when he was a long way away and could not possibly be in a position to help.

Now all that Margaret had left was the portrait of Harry, painted by Zephanaiah Bell. Mr. Denniston, a Railway Engineer, had kindly brought it down from London, and Margaret received it on 16th May 1849, five months after Harry sat for it. It had cost ten guineas, with another £2.10.0 for the frame and the packing.

Margaret was pleased to have it, but was not entirely satisfied with it:

"It certainly is a very good likeness of your face, dearest Harry, but looking so very grave! I think the colour of your face is too dark and the hair a deeper shade of auburn than it really is. Bell has painted you sitting in a very easy but rather slouching position on a balustrade on a terrace, with a beautiful forest in the background. The position would have done well for Jem, but is not upright enough for you. The limbs look rather large, but just as they looked in those thick grey trousers; they would have looked much smarter in your military ones. However poor Bell had not a fair chance, as he only saw you in uniform for such a short time, and we were so hurried altogether."

The portrait shows Harry in his scarlet coatee and black winter trousers, his new Lieutenant's epaulettes, a red sash and his sword in the buff leather belt and frog, which he preferred to the black leather belt with slings. He is holding his chaco, as he invariably spelt it, with the 64th badge and red tuft, on his knee.

Margaret had recently been talking to Bennett Hubbard, a well-known Louth artist, who told her that he knew Zephanaiah Bell, having frequently met him at conversaziones in London, and that he was better known as a painter of Classical groups, than of portraits. In Hubbard's opinion Bell's use of colour was harsh, and not always able to stand a close inspection, as his own could. *"This was all delivered*

Detail from the Cure-all painting by Hubbard, showing Kitty Crisp, the Healing groom, and a great ally of Harry and Jem.

in the most conceited manner, and with so much pomposity and strutting about, that I nearly laughed out loud. But then, as you know, that is always his manner."

In spite of his manner, Margaret rather regretted the portrait could not have been painted by Hubbard, who had produced a striking likeness of Harry's grandfather, old General Loft, as well as smaller portraits of William Loft and Crisp in a painting of Cure-all. All her friends gave their opinion of it. Uncle Fred thought Harry's portrait *"quite good but too old and grand looking"*, while Gloriana, his wife, did not like it at all. Edmund Smyth considered it to be passable, while Dr. Banks roundly declared, *"Bell has not made him half such a good looking fellow as he really is"*. Margaret's old Scottish servant, Jane, was of much the same opinion, *"which is a wonder for her to acknowledge"*. Harry's friend, Faulk Allison came to see it, and thought it a good likeness, but that it looked better at a distance.

The person who approved of it most highly was Harry's brother, James, who thought it *"a capital likeness, and the exact image of you."* He would listen to no criticism of it and insisted that it should be hung on the dining room wall, opposite his chair, so that he could look at it, and talk to it, while he ate his meals. It continued to be one of his treasured possessions all his life.

Margaret continued to take an interest in the Regiment. She heard of the gallant death of Colonel James Stopford, leading the Regiment into action at Reshire in the Persian campaign of 1856, an almost forgotten incident in the Great Game played between the British Empire and Tsarist Russia. Each nation was anxious to prevent the other from acquiring a base in Afghanistan, and Persia, not for the last time, was caught up between the two powers. Soon afterwards she learned with great regret of the death from fever of Captain James, Harry's friend and Company Commander, at Hyderabad in 1851. This must have been a difficult time for the 64th, as both Surgeon Archer and Assistant Surgeon Short also died of fever in the same place within a few months of each other.

A few years later Margaret had a further reminder of the past when the 64th, was engaged in the bitter battles of the Indian Mutiny, and formed part of the column, which struggled to relieve Cawnpore and Lucknow in fearful conditions with bitter fighting under Henry Havelock.

12th September 1857

"Do you see how gallantly the 64th and the 78th, Tom Anderson's Regt., have been acting under General Havelock, at Futtockpore. This news brings the ache back to my heart, as I remember all the sadness we have known in our lives, and the regrets at what might have been, if God had decreed otherwise. I was glad to see from the Military Gazette that the poor 64th has not suffered quite so much as was at first stated, with General Windham. A letter says 'the gallant 64th most pressingly volunteered to go to Lucknow, but all to no purpose. The Headquarters of some Regiment must be stationed here (Cawnpore) *and it has fallen to your lot, brave 64th,' was the answer received from Sir Colin Campbell."*

With pride she read of some of Harry's contemporaries, of Lieut. Alfred Bowlby's distinguished conduct, and with sorrow of the deaths of Thomas Sterling, whose coat Harry had borrowed to go on guard in Cork and of Captain Richard Macrae, with whom he had exchanged postings. With relief she heard of the Regiment's eventual safe return to England, just ten years after Harry had sailed with it from Cork. The Colonel, Charles William Sibley, died almost immediately after their return, as a result of his service in the Mutiny, and Harry's old friend, Neville Shute, was promoted to the vacant command, without purchase, and retired as a Colonel in 1869. Another of his friends, Mockler, became the senior Major, and Bingham went on half pay as Lieutenant Colonel in 1861.

Margaret wrote to James about her feelings, with her usual ability to look on the bright side. *"It is with a sad heart that I read these accounts tho' I ought to be thankful not to have the dreadful anxiety under which so many are suffering. But we must be thankful that together we have so much to enjoy in the present."*

Margaret Boswell Loft died at her house in Ramsgate, in Lincolnshire, in April 1860, at the age of 50. She was buried at Healing beside her husband, who had died 30 years previously.

However, one of Margaret's dearest wishes had been granted. She had done everything in her power to secure Jem a place at Corpus Christi College, Cambridge, and she lived long enough to see him, now officially the Reverend J.E.Wallis Loft, inducted as Rector of Healing, the place of his birth, living in a brand new Rectory. It was one of the very first of a great many such houses to be designed by James Fowler of Louth. To Margaret's regret, and in spite of all her matchmaking efforts, he was still a bachelor. It was not for another three years that he married Margaret Jane Trotter of Bishop Auckland, the sister of one of his Cambridge friends.

Healing saw many changes. Before Uncle Fred and his new wife took up residence there, she had insisted that something more modern must replace the old furniture that had been in the House since it was built in the eighteenth century. Everything in the house and the garden, and the daily routine was to reflect Victorian fashions and attitudes rather than to follow the carefree Georgian and Regency style that had predominated previously.

Sadly, when Uncle Fred died in 1876, the wife of his eldest son, Alfred, had an exaggerated idea of her husband's wealth, and she began a spending spree. Once again everything was replaced by new furniture in the latest ornate fashion, and the family adopted an even more luxurious life style. Within six years the house was mortgaged and then everything was sold at knockdown prices. Over the years it deteriorated, and finally was divided into three cottages, which by 1965 were so dilapidated that they were demolished.

Jem continued as the Rector of Healing until 1880 when he became Rector of Swallow. He stayed there, in another of James Fowler's houses, until his death in 1909, aged 78. A well-known and much loved figure, he continued to lead a very active sporting life, shooting, fishing, following the Brocklesby Hunt, playing cricket and football, refereeing and umpiring. He umpired a cricket match in Grimsby four days before his death. He was disappointed by his failure to establish a successful Lincolnshire County Cricket Club, but was proud to have played for a Grimsby team against W.G. Grace's Eleven, even though *"Grace kept the Grimbarians leather-chasing for three days"* as the local paper described it. He was the Chairman of the Caistor Board of Guardians until the Local Government Act, when he became the first Chairman of the Caistor Rural District Council. He was also Rural Dean of Grimsby, and for many years President of the Louth Grammar School Old Boys' Association. In spite of his dread of the Headmaster while he was a schoolboy, a portrait of John Waite hung on his study wall, and, of course, Harry's portrait hung in the dining room.

Jem and his wife had three sons and one daughter. All four of their children inherited their father's sporting interests. At one time he and his sons were all Captains of their local cricket clubs, in Caistor, Grimsby, Bishop Auckland, and Stourport-on-Severn respectively, while their sister played in Lady Yarborough's Eleven against Lady Heneage's Eleven. Two of his sons married daughters of Harry's old friend 'Faulk' Allison, who was a solicitor, Town Clerk of Louth for many years, and a prominent figure in the religious, educational and philanthropic life of the town, where his portrait hangs in the Town Hall. Harry's other great friend, Charley Banks, who had been the despair of his father for his scapegrace ways, became a barrister, Sub-Treasurer and Steward of Gray's Inn, and Secretary of the Land Court of Mauritius.

Five generations of Margaret Loft's descendants have lived in Louth, and three generations still do.

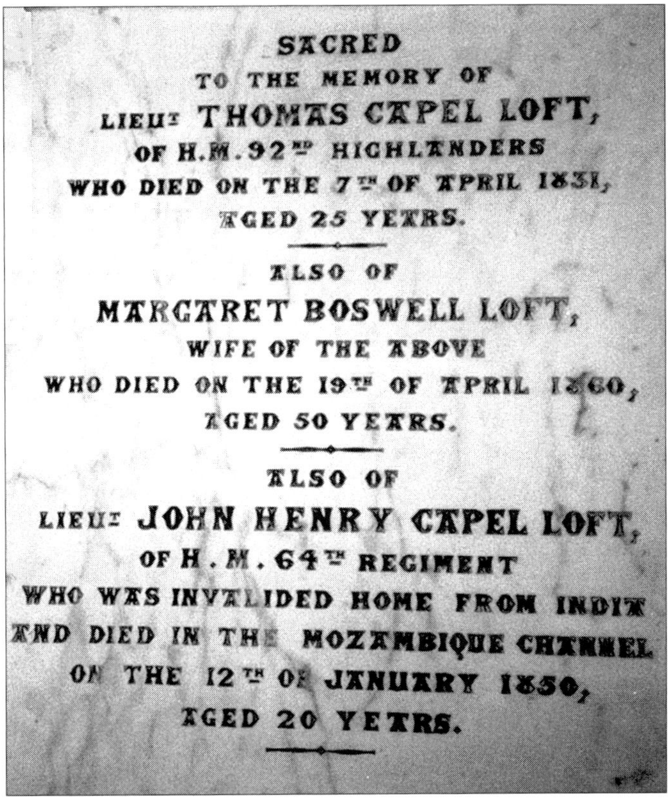

The monument in Healing Church, which Jem Loft erected in memory of his parents and brother when he was Rector of Healing.

The grave stones of Thomas and Margaret Loft in Healing churchyard, where many other Lofts are buried.

Harry's Regimental Belt plate,
returned to his mother after his death.